About the author

The author at home working on his next book

Kevin Wraight is an historian with a keen interest for naval warfare. His first two books are *War at Sea* and *Battlefleet and Empire — A Brief History of the Royal Navy 1588 to 1922*. Alongside a successful career in business Kevin has been studying military history for over thirty years and his enthusiasm for the subject knows no bounds. In his own words Kevin wishes to "pass on my enthusiasm to the readers of my books and I hope they are both informed and entertained." Kevin was born in North London in 1971 and now resides in Devon.

BATTLEFLEET AND EMPIRE

KEVIN WRAIGHT

BATTLEFLEET AND EMPIRE

Vanguard Press

VANGUARD PAPERBACK

© Copyright 2022
Kevin Wraight

The right of Kevin Wraight to be identified as author of
this work has been asserted by him in accordance with the
Copyright, Designs and Patents Act 1988.

All Rights Reserved

No reproduction, copy or transmission of this publication
may be made without written permission.
No paragraph of this publication may be reproduced,
copied or transmitted save with the written permission of the
publisher, or in accordance with the provisions
of the Copyright Act 1956 (as amended).

Any person who commits any unauthorised act in relation to
this publication may be liable to criminal
prosecution and civil claims for damages.

A CIP catalogue record for this title is
available from the British Library.

ISBN 978 1 80016 164 1

Vanguard Press is an imprint of
Pegasus Elliot MacKenzie Publishers Ltd.
www.pegasuspublishers.com

First Published in 2022

Vanguard Press
Sheraton House Castle Park
Cambridge England

Printed & Bound in Great Britain

Dedication

To all men and women of the Royal Navy,
past, present and future.

Contents

Forward 11
Introduction 13
The Early Navy to the Spanish Armada 15
Disaster and Triumph — 1588 to 1700 30
The Race for Empire — 1700 to 1775 46
Revolution and Liberation — 1775 to 1815 69
The Age of Iron and Steam — 1815 to 1914 111
The Beginning of the End of Empire 1914 to 1922 125
Epilogue 160
Glossary 164
INDEX 171

'The Navy, whereon under the good providence of God the wealth, safety and strength of the Kingdom chiefly depend.'
Preamble to The Articles of War

Forward

Many books have been written on the subject of the Royal Navy, all with their own unique purpose and intentions. Some of these highlight the many battle honours of this renowned force, many the organisation in war and peace time and yet still more works focusing on the people and human face of the service throughout history.

The purpose of this book is to tell a story. What I want to achieve is a piece of work that shows how the Royal Navy adapted to meet circumstances and events without losing its essential foundations of tradition, honour and duty, foundations that have been centuries in the building. Also, it is my intention to show how the Royal Navy was instrumental in building an empire.

It has been said that the Royal Navy was at times a backward thinking organisation steeped in the old ways. These criticisms have been levelled at the organisation from time to time however it should be remembered that the Royal Navy has ever been the initiator of technological and tactical advances. From the introduction of fighting instructions, coppering of wooden sailing ships and the tactic of splitting the enemy line of battle to the invention of the steam catapult for aircraft carriers the Royal Navy has been at the forefront of technological achievement.

This is a concise history and the size of the work reflects that but I hope I will highlight the salient points in the development of the navy and how the navy helped create the empire. However, in the course of this narrative other important aspects will of necessity be omitted simply to allow space. This is not meant just as a chronological history of the Royal Navy, it is to show how certain events shaped the navy and the world. I hope the reader enjoys absorbing this book as much as I have enjoyed researching and writing it.

This brief history will tell the unique story of the Royal Navy through some of its darkest and most successful times. We will discover together how the Royal Navy formed its traditions and carried out its ever-changing role in an ever-changing world. We will see how it faced up to and defeated enemies abroad and often enemies close to home who wished to strip the navy of its fighting potential through budget cuts. Above all we will see how the Royal Navy shaped the modern world and forged and protected the largest empire in history.

Kevin Wraight, Stoke Canon, 1st May 2020

Introduction

'Oh God, thy sea is so great and my boat is so small'
Part of a Breton Fisherman's Prayer

No subject in military history has more interest to me than sea power and its effect on history. Of course one cannot study sea power and its effects without studying the Royal Navy. In the late 19th century an American naval officer Alfred Thayer Mahan wrote a book titled 'The Influence of Sea Power on History'. In his book he described that quite simply the nation which commanded a large blue water battle fleet could control and maintain an empire rich in commerce. In simple terms a navy will give a much better return on investment than an army because it can both promote and secure trade whilst projecting that nation's influence over a far larger area internationally. Mahan was of course absolutely correct in his writing and indeed his book prompted the United States to build and maintain a large fleet prior to World War I. It is no accident that at the turn of the 21st century the USA is not only the world's largest trading nation but it also commands the largest navy, however China is fast catching up on both these counts. At the turn of the 20th

century, it was of course Britain that carried this accolade and had done for a hundred years.

It could be argued that Mahan was simply stating the obvious and in hindsight it certainly seems that way, however he was the first to document what had in effect been the story of Britain and her empire jealously guarded by the Royal Navy. One person who took Mahan's writing seriously was Kaiser Wilhelm II. An industrious empire builder he wanted more than anything to emulate Great Britain and her empire. We will see in more detail later how this emperor was to play his part in creating the bloodiest century in the history of the world to date, and the Royal Navy's part in defeating him.

So how did this small island on the fringe of the European continent come to practice so effectively what Mahan has sought to quantify? It is of course a mixture of things — timing, leadership, love of exploration, courage, daring, greed and scientific endeavour. But primarily it is due to Britain being an island astride the key sea routes of the western hemisphere, an island which furthermore contains some of the finest natural harbours in the world. But most importantly being an island there are no land borders so unlike other European states vast expenditure on an army was not required which allowed Britain to turn to the sea in order to shape her destiny.

The Early Navy to the Spanish Armada

The first recordings of a national navy in England go back to the days of King Alfred in the 9th century. Here the navy was formed as a line of defence against Viking aggression and on the face of it appears to have been quite effective at times and certainly held its own against the Vikings.

The Anglo-Saxon Chronicle gives an illuminating account of this navy describing how King Alfred designed ships specifically to take on and defeat the Vikings describing them as being *'...nearly twice as long as the others......Also higher than the others; nor were they in the Frisian manner or the Danish but as he (Alfred) thought might be most useful'*

In 897 the fledgling navy met the Danes in battle somewhere near Poole and defeated them.

Unfortunately, this is where the first instances of funding and other financial commitments rear their collective heads in the story of the Royal Navy. When the threat to England had passed the navy was disbanded and the ships put into commerce. For over five hundred years, it remained that warships, were only ever to be commercial vessels which were armed and seconded in time of war.

Throughout the period until the early 16th century the collection of ships for purposes of war was known as the '*Navy Royal*'. The Navy Royal was specific to task in that it was the amalgamation of shipping for the purpose of war. Usually this meant collecting ships in order to transport an army. After this task was completed, the ships would disperse. In 1295 there was the first recording of the position of Lord Admiral. The word admiral is Arabic in origin and the title was clearly borrowed from the sea powers of the Mediterranean. In the context of the Navy Royal the title of Lord Admiral was solely administrative and the holder of the title was concerned with the assembling and supply of a fleet in time of war. In peace time the Lord Admiral dealt with disputes between ship owners, thus making the position very profitable and highly sought after.

The actual tactical command of the Navy Royal was held by a 'Captain', a land army term which highlights the nature of sea warfare at this time. It very much mirrored warfare on land with ships coming together so that soldiers may fight as they would on land. In this respect little had changed since Roman times when during the Punic Wars the Romans developed the use of the *Corvus* as a means of boarding from ship to ship.

The major naval confrontations of this time for England were during the Hundred Years War between

England and France. During this bloody conflagration the English used ships to convey armies to France which proved decisive on the battlefield, a perfect example of using sea power to further a land commitment and carry it through to a successful conclusion. During this war we also see the use by French forces of ships to raid the English coast, most notably the attacks on Plymouth and North Devon in 1377 and 1400 respectively by a mixture of French ships and Genoese galleys. This is where that great harbour of Plymouth comes to the fore as in 1356 The Black Prince embarked his army from there for France and his subsequent victories in the Loire.

After this time the most momentous events occurred during the reign of Henry VIII. Famous of course for his marital affairs he could certainly be described as the father of the Royal Navy and as a king he laid the foundations of what was to become the most successful navy in the history of the world. When Henry disbanded the monasteries after his split from the Church of Rome a great deal of money fell into the royal treasury and Henry was quick to use this on the navy. In this work I do not want to look too closely at individual ships however it is important to look at ship types and the building of fighting vessels. Henry was heavily committed to large, purpose-built warships. Until this time fighting at sea was undertaken by merchant ships such as carracks which were commandeered and fitted out for war. Henry began to build a series of purpose-built battleships such as the *Great Harry, Peter Pomegranate* and *Mary Rose*. The *Mary Rose* can be described as the first purpose-built ship of battle as she encompassed revolutionary sealed gun ports which allowed her to fire broadsides. These ships were heavily gunned vessels with a large crew, not just of seamen but of fighting soldiers also. Throughout this time and indeed the age of sail the purpose of a fight at sea was mainly to board and capture enemy ships as this ultimately saved money in ship building, also it is very hard to sink a wooden warship. These battleships were very successful and were instrumental in keeping England's traditional enemy France in check.

In 1545 war broke out against France and Scotland simultaneously and this saw Henry use his fleet to first sail north and raid Edinburgh and Leith then back south to meet a French invasion fleet in the Solent off the Isle of Wight. It was in this action that the great warship the *Mary Rose*, pride of the fleet, sank with virtually all hands. Very likely due to being overloaded and top heavy with her lower gun ports awash rather than enemy action. Despite the tragic loss the English fleet did defeat the French force and cause them to return to France, thus preventing invasion.

Naval administration and organisation for war was further improved when in 1549 Henry formed the Navy Board, England being the first nation to do so. The board's duties were to standardise the operations of the dockyards and oversee the construction and maintenance of warships.

The Mary Rose

However, to my mind there was a far more influential occurrence that was to prove vital to England's seafaring future and that was the fall of Calais in 1558. This one act finally ended the seesaw wars on the continent between England and France and as a consequence turned England away from a continental aspiration and forced her to look to the sea as a means of gaining power and influence and even more importantly it laid down a tradition of sea faring which came to life during the golden age of Henry's daughter Elizabeth I. Here we take up the story with the wars against Spain and the Spanish Armada.

In this period, we see great mariners such as Drake, Hawkins, Raleigh and Frobisher sailing the seas of the world promoting English power, raiding Spanish shipping (which was a huge boost to the English economy), founding new lands such as Virginia in the Americas and most importantly honing the skills of seamanship which were to prove so vital in the centuries to come. England's mariners were to come into contact with Spain many times during the latter half of the 16th century. There were numerous attacks on Spanish shipping and colonies which coupled with the Protestant religion in England was to lead inevitably to open conflict with Spain.

Spain of course had set herself up as the protector of the Catholic Church and took a keen interest in the plight of Catholics in England. Elizabeth was all for free religious practices, however all the plots against her appear to have been Catholic in origin when uncovered by Elizabeth's master spy Francis Walsingham. There was also at this time a great drive within England to convert intellectuals to Catholicism and the religion was going from strength to strength. In the eyes of Philip II the internal English religious dispute was brought to a head with the execution of Mary Queen of Scots after it was proved she was openly plotting to usurp the throne of England. Mary had rather foolishly and naively been involved in a plot constructed by Walsingham and involving the merchant, Anthony Babington. This execution coupled with the practice of Catholicism eventually being made illegal in England was all the religious ammunition Philip needed to justify war with Elizabeth's England.

Philip saw this war as a crusade and openly sought the support of Pope Sixtus V but the Pope set certain conditions on his support. These were to have a dramatic effect on the success of the armada and can even provide the reason for the failure. Spain's other concerns were the blatant attacks on her shipping by English gentlemen mariners and privateers. These were made worse by the fact that the queen openly encouraged the attacks and indeed profited by them both personally and for the nation. At this time England was also openly assisting the Protestant Dutch in their fight against Catholic Spain, so a formal clash of arms was inevitable. Thus, Philip II of Spain finally decided in 1586 to embark on the 'enterprise of England'.

In 1586 Philip turned to the Marquis of Santa Cruz, his most able military strategist and instructed him to form a plan for the invasion of England. Santa Cruz's plan was perfect in its conception and had this been the plan that was followed would most likely have succeeded. Santa Cruz decided that an army of fifty-five thousand soldiers transported by a fleet of eighty thousand tons and escorted by six galleasses (a cross between a galleon and a galley), forty galleys and two hundred landing craft should sail to South East England and land in Kent as a prelude to an attack on London.

However, this plan could not be followed due to the conditions set by Pope Sixtus V. He was not willing to make this a political or territorial gain for Spain and certainly not an attempt to extend the empire. Therefore, his condition was that the army employed must be led by the Duke of Parma, an Italian (albeit nephew of Philip II) who was conducting the land campaign against the protestant Dutch in what was considered a religious war. This changed the strategy completely and meant that a compromise of the Santa Cruz plan was required. This revised plan was that the fleet would have to sail to the Low Countries, rendezvous with and embark Parma's army, then carry out a landing on the south coast of England. Santa Cruz was furious at this revised plan and quite rightly pointed out the flaws and dangers connected with it. His main concerns were that the fleet would have to sail up channel and then attempt to meet with an army and embark it in Dutch waters where the Dutch Navy was well versed in fighting, all this whilst fighting off the English Navy. Philip's mind however was made up, this was the plan engaged and thus were sown the seeds of failure.

The building up of the armada began in earnest with the requisitioning and building of ships. This of course takes time and the attrition suffered by the armada was a constant drain on its resources, a situation not helped by Drake's pre-emptive strike on Cadiz in 1587 which destroyed much materiel and caused the expedition to be put back a year. In January 1588 Santa Cruz, worn out by his service died. Philip chose as his successor the Duke of Medina Sidonia, Spain's foremost nobleman and an able military commander.

The English fleet assembled on the south coast to meet this threat was quite a bit different to the Spanish fleet. It must be remembered that the English had been used to attacking Spanish vessels for some time whereas the Spanish ships and crews were more used to convoy escort. This gave the English a distinct edge which was increased by the use of a remarkable English ship design, the race-built galleon. Far different to the large battleships built by Henry VIII these ships were built for speed and for the use of heavy artillery. The race-built galleon was so named from the term *raised* to denote the raised fore and aft castles.

Defence of the Revenge, a race built galleon

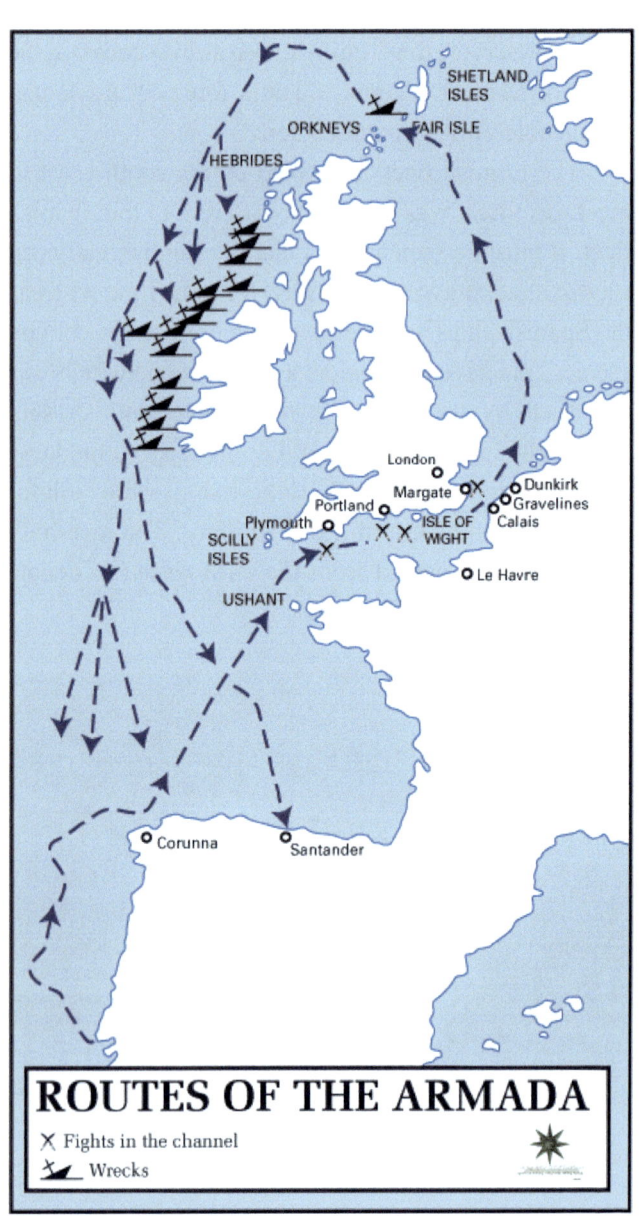

Ironically the preparedness of the English fleet was very much down to the organisational skills of Philip himself. He was after all King of England from 1554 to 1558 whilst married to Queen Mary. Whilst in this position he administered the English Navy and turned it around from the sorry bankrupt state it was left in by Henry. Also at this crucial time the Navy Board was headed by that great seafarer John Hawkins. He was instrumental in preparing the navy for the coming fight and built the first ever dry dock at Deptford on the Medway. The English also possessed the best cannon at this time, they were iron rather than bronze and although bronze was widely recognised to be superior to iron it was much more expensive. However English iron ore possessed certain mineral properties which rendered the iron far stronger and more flexible than iron from other regions, thus making the cannon almost as good as the bronze pieces but much cheaper and easier to produce.

On 28th May1588, the fleet sailed from Lisbon arriving off Ushant in late July. It then began its run up the Channel arrayed in a crescent formation with divisions to the left and right ready to sally out and engage any enemy that presented itself.

The English Admiral Lord Howard of Effingham had sought the advice of Francis Drake over fleet deployment and Drake advised that the fleet station itself in Plymouth, for two reasons:

1. It can protect the West Country which could be a potential landing zone.
2. More importantly, it gave the English the weather gauge, essential in any battle at this time, especially with the prevailing south westerly winds.

The armada sailed slowly up channel and the English fleet slipped in neatly behind it. There then began the bombardment of the Spanish ships by the English with ships individually sallying forth, firing and then returning to formation. The Spanish flank guards could not intercept these as it meant sailing into the wind, so the Spanish fleet had to endure this punishment. However, the bombardment did not do a great deal of damage to the Spanish ships and the English were quite rightly concerned about how to stop this vast fleet. It was Drake who provided the first major victory of the ongoing sea fight when he captured the *Nuestra Seniora Del Rosario*. Admittedly he was after treasure and had indeed disobeyed orders but it was an important victory all the same in that it provided intelligence on the handling of the guns in Spanish ships and showed that it could take up to a day to reload.

The Spanish fleet uncertain of the location of Parma's army anchored off Calais and sent riders to find Parma. This presented the English with the perfect opportunity to use fire ships which they sent in under cover of darkness with a strong prevailing wind. The resultant chaos and panic inflicted on the Spanish caused most of the armada to cut its moorings and scatter. Medina Sidonia and the bulk of the fighting ships regrouped the scattered fleet and moved further up the coast into Dutch waters pursued by the English still bombarding them.

At this critical stage the armada found itself off Gravelines where they were engaged again in earnest by the English. Many Spanish ships were damaged and a few were sunk or run aground but the armada remained intact, however the effect on Spanish moral was hugely deleterious. Had the armada been the self-contained force that Santa Cruz had insisted on then it could have landed the army in southern England days ago without any opposition. However, the armada found itself off a hostile coast and no army in sight. Medina Sidonia realised he could not remain where he was for fear of more fire ships so in the absence of Parma, he had no choice but to keep moving. This meant inevitably north and into the gales of the North Sea. The English (out of ammunition) pursued the Spanish fleet as far as the coast of lowland Scotland where it broke off pursuit. As the Armada made its way round Scotland and Ireland it lost ships on the hazardous coastlines of those countries until the tired and diseased crews finally found their way back to Spain.

The war with Spain provided vast amounts of money and treasure for the national economy but more importantly it was a successful and moral boosting enterprise for English sailors and ships. Not only do we see the fight against the armada but also countless smaller actions involving the capture of Spanish treasure ships and the highly successful raid on Cádiz carried out by Drake in 1587. The destruction of the armada was to lead to bankruptcy for Spain on the death of the Spanish King Philip II in 1599 and this allowed England to supplant Spain as the world's leading naval power.

After the defeat of the armada English mariners were able to exploit the victory by sailing further into the south seas where they broke in to the lucrative Spanish and Portuguese trade with India and the Far East. This culminated with Raleigh's capture of the Portuguese galleon *Madre De Deus* in August 1592 and with it much treasure and wealth. Far more important though was the seizure of the ship's rutter or mariner's handbook. The rutter (a precursor to charts) contained sailing directions and navigation information of the trade routes to the countries of the Far East such as Japan and China.

On 31st December 1600, the East India Company was officially formed with the intention of sending trade ships to the Far East which it did every year for the next sixteen years. The company also established trading posts ashore in India in 1612 and Japan in 1613. These laid the foundations for one of the most successful and richest trade companies of the age and began the road to empire for Britain. The East India Company would come to dominate India entirely with its private army and navy and provide one of the wealthiest sources of trade for the British Empire.

Therefore, when we consider the episode of the armada we should not perhaps think only in terms of the long tenacious channel fight and the subsequent destruction of the Spanish fleet but also of the effect on the history of the world as a consequence. The failure of the armada is for me one of the pivotal maritime moments which has shaped the world. It could be argued that without the defeat of the armada and subsequent bankruptcy of Spain, England may not actually have emerged as the world power she became. The war with Spain saw the decline of one empire and the rise of another, a pattern constantly repeated in history but never before in a purely maritime sense with little land combat. The best quote to sum this up is from the great mariner, Sir Walter Raleigh, who said: "Whoever commands the sea, commands the trade; whosoever commands the trade of the world, commands the riches of the world, and consequently, the world itself."

Disaster and Triumph — 1588 to 1700

After the death of Elizabeth, the navy underwent a large period of stagnation under her nephew James I. Sadly he was more interested in his own lavish lifestyle than the protection and expansion of Britain through her navy. James was a notorious spender of money and under his monarchy we see vast expenditure on building works and royal banquets.

However, under James I we see the beginnings of the union of England and Scotland and the joint enterprise of trade. This led to a decline in the fighting navy with ships being left idle and unkempt. But periods such as this are never a bad thing in naval history. After World War I the German fleet was scuttled which meant that during the Nazi resurgence ships could be built and designed with all modern aspects, whereas existing ships that were decades old were simply refitted. The same applies to the Royal Navy under James's son Charles I. After years of neglect by his father Charles commissioned a new fighting ship, *Sovereign of the Seas*. The largest warship ever built in Britain up to that time she was to become the blueprint for all line of battleships to come in the age of sail.

With the coming of Charles I to the throne the navy became a key factor in English policy making both home and abroad. In 1625 an abortive attempt to raid Cadiz led to a rethink on how to organise and run a navy. For the first time during this raid ships were led into battle in squadrons each led by an admiral, vice admiral and rear admiral respectively and each given a colour to signify the squadron. This in turn led to the adoption of ranks such as Admiral of the Red, Blue etc. In 1634 Charles introduced the controversial Ship Money tax which would begin the steady decline into eventual Civil War but was at first a godsend to the navy. By 1635 there were twenty-four warships of various kinds patrolling the English Channel and protecting the coast from North African pirates who had sailed freely around the southern half of Britain raiding and taking away slaves, indeed whole villages and towns were sometimes wiped off the map and depopulated. Ship Money also led to the fulltime employment of professional officers, a vast step forward.

Under Charles we also see the beginnings of what was to be the famed ship of the line that was to serve the navies of all nations so well in the coming two hundred years. In 1637 the *Sovereign of the Seas* was launched. Boasting three decks and one hundred guns she was both master of the oceans and a political statement. As history records the English Civil War put paid to Charles and during the war the sea was not a battleground exploited by either side except to blockade certain ports. Few major fleet actions took place but command of the ports by parliament was a key economic factor in final victory.

Sovereign of the Seas.

By 1653 after the civil war the navy mustered one hundred and thirty-three warships, the largest full-time navy in the world. This force consisted of a mixture of ships of the line and the fast and well gunned *fregets* of Spanish design, (more commonly called frigates by the British). The ships were commanded by four generals of the sea who had been successful generals on land during the Civil War fighting for parliament against the king. These were Popham, Deane and most famously Blake and Monk. During the period of the Commonwealth the navy under these men again took its place in helping to shape Britain and its future and was at the forefront of a set of vicious though productive and significant conflagrations known collectively as the Anglo-Dutch Wars.

The Anglo-Dutch wars were a series of wars fought between the English and the Dutch in the 17th century for control over the seas and trade routes. The main reason for this set of unfortunate wars was the passing of the Navigation Acts through Parliament in England. These acts were designed to protect Commonwealth trade by only allowing goods to be landed in England and her territories by English merchant ships. This was clearly aimed at the Dutch who at that time had the largest merchant fleet in the world and was an attempt to control the lucrative maritime trade through the English Channel. There is no doubt that the English were spoiling for a fight with the Dutch because on top of the Navigation Acts the English also began insisting that foreign vessels pay respects to English ships by lowering their colours when they passed at sea. On 29th May 1652 the Dutch Admiral Maarten Tromp refused to dip his colours to an English fleet commanded by Admiral Blake in the Channel resulting in a skirmish known as the Battle of Goodwin Sands after which the English formally declared war on 10th July.

This sharp action was followed in September by a skirmish off the Kentish Knock. This battle was the first time in which the line of battle was used by Blake giving the ships the ability to fire full broadsides using movable guns into the enemy and as time went on led to removing the guns in the fore and aft of the ship and reducing them to chasers. There was a further engagement in November off Dungeness where the English fleet holding the weather gauge had a good chance to engage in line of battle and cause much damage to the Dutch fleet, however many ship's captains refused to engage. This led to Blake writing his dictum on naval warfare *'The Laws of war and Ordinances of the Sea'* which in turn led to the introduction of the Articles of War in 1652. These were Rules of engagement laid down for ships captains containing no ambiguity. You will follow the orders of the officer in charge or be court martialled. As extreme and bizarre as this now sounds to us leaving no room for independent thought it was vital in ensuring that the ships could inflict maximum damage on the enemy. The articles governed all aspects of navy life for the common seaman as well as the officers. Thirteen, of the thirty-nine articles listed called for the punishment of death to those who transgressed the laws.

They proved their worth in 1653 when on 2nd June, an English fleet engaged a Dutch fleet off Harwich sinking or capturing twenty ships without loss. This was followed by the Battle of Scheveningen on 31st July 1653, where Monk defeated a Dutch fleet commanded by Tromp and sunk, captured or crippled thirty ships, killing Tromp in the process. The war ended in April 1654 with England very much in the ascendant, however the Dutch would be back in less than ten years with larger more powerfully armed warships.

Mention needs to be made here of Oliver Cromwell. He must take full credit for bringing the Dutch fleet to its knees in the first Anglo-Dutch war. For better or worse he unified England, secured the sea lanes for trade and created a navy that was second to none in the world at that time. Cromwell also appointed the Generals at Sea, Blake and Monk who were so significant in England's naval victories at this time.

At the end of the First Anglo-Dutch War the navy was put into peace time mode, however this was still ruinously expensive costing around £450,000 a year, half the annual income. In 1664 war flared up again between England and The Netherlands with an attempt by the English to corner more lucrative trade routes in order to reduce the exchequer's dependency on parliament for raising funds. Squadrons were sent south to capture Dutch colonies in Africa and across the Atlantic to secure the vitally important port of New Amsterdam (now New York) in the Americas whilst the bulk of the navy concentrated at Portsmouth ready to engage the Dutch in what was hoped to be a decisive battle. This was the first instance of the use of the Duke of York and Albany's Maritime Regiment of Foot, soon to become known as the Admiral's Regiment and eventually as the Royal Marines. This regiment was formed to fight on board ship and be used to board and capture enemy vessels. It also gave the navy a unique force that could operate ashore with all the skill and discipline of an army, vital in securing and controlling events on land.

In mid-June 1665, the Dutch fleet of one hundred and three ships sallied forth into the North Sea in order to prevent a blockade of their coast by the Royal Navy (the navy was designated Royal Navy by Charles II on his restoration in1660) under Charles's brother James Duke of York with one hundred and nine ships. On 13th June the fleets met off Lowestoft where a decisive action was won by the Royal Navy. Whilst engaged, the Dutch ships failed to keep in line of battle and overlapped each other which reduced the ability to have all guns bearing on the English ships.

The tactic and discipline of the Royal Navy's fighting instructions proved their worth in the battle as opposed to the Dutch fleet which contained many Dutch East India Company ships that were especially guilty of not following signals and instructions, not surprising as they were not trained or instructed in fleet actions. As a consequence of this poor command and lack of ability the English surrounded the Dutch fleet and destroyed or captured seventeen ships for the loss of only one English ship, a stunning victory for the time. The English however failed to follow up this victory by not going on to blockade the Dutch coast and as a consequence a rich East India Fleet made its way safely to Dutch ports despite an attempt to capture it at the Battle of Vagen on the 2nd August.

By this time and prior to the battle off Lowestoft the navy was fast running out of funds. Some ships were up to forty percent down on manpower and mutiny was reported. The government had decided not to pay sailors in full in order to prevent desertion and this whole sorry episode came to a head in 1667 when after the Great Fire of London funds for the navy were at an all-time low. The Clerk to the Acts of the Navy Board Samuel Pepys and his Navy Board staff were besieged in their temporary offices in the former Royal Palace at Greenwich (having moved there to avoid the worst of the plague) by angry sailors demanding payment and the fleet was laid up at Chatham. Here follows one of the most embarrassing and disastrous episodes in Royal Navy history, the raid on the Medway.

On 22nd June 1667, a Dutch fleet sailed up the Medway to the English fleet at anchor and began bombarding and cutting out ships. Shore defences and batteries were powerless to intervene due to a lack of both manpower and ordnance. Indeed, in some cases shore batteries were unable to fire as the balls were too big for the guns. The Dutch sailed away with barely a scratch on any man or ship leaving three ships burning and the pride of the Royal Navy the *Royal Charles* captured and being taken back down the Medway to Dutch waters. In all the fleet lost six ships including a one hundred gun and two, eighty gun line of battle ships.

Despite this humiliation the English did come out on top in the second Anglo-Dutch War. The Dutch were exhausted as a nation and had lost a great many ships and a good deal of wealth. At the signing of the Treaty of Breda the Dutch did regain some lost outposts in the West Indies and some concessions to the Navigation Acts but on the whole, they faired rather badly. The English secured bases in North America and Africa from the Dutch and most important of all the English East India Company was moved to Bombay where it would base itself astride the routes to the Indian subcontinent and the lucrative Far East trade.

The third war fought between April 1672 and February 1674 was a much less conclusive war for England. Charles II had formed an alliance with France in the hope of finishing the Dutch for good and the war started with the English and French fleets unsuccessfully blockading the Dutch coast. This was followed by the Battle of Southwold Bay on 7th June 1672. The Dutch fleet under De Ruyter engaged the English fleet under James Duke of York. It was a tactical English victory in that the Dutch lost five ships to England's one, but the English fleet was very badly battered and unable to take offensive action and follow up the victory. Also, the French fleet did not join battle as expected putting pressure on the already shaky alliance. This could well have been a cynical attempt by the French to have the two premiere naval powers fight it out and weaken each other, then step in afterwards to gain control of the seas.

Three more actions were fought off the Dutch coast in the following year or so but the English and French were unable to blockade the Dutch coast. The French were also unable to carry out their planned land attack on The Netherlands due to deliberate flooding of the land by the Dutch. Charles was eventually forced to withdraw Britain from the war due to lack of funds and pressure from parliament over the suspicion and fear that the alliance with France would influence a road back for the Catholic faith.

The Anglo-Dutch wars were to prove a costly venture for England but there were major benefits. The English certainly came out on top in terms of the use of strategy and tactics. The line of battle system proved the way forward for another century and more importantly England supplanted the Dutch as the main European traders with the beginnings of an oversea empire. At the end of the wars, we see England strongly settled in North America, South Africa and most significant of all in India.

Of course no study of naval matters in this period can be complete without a look at the contribution of Samuel Pepys. He is famous of course for his diaries which are an illuminating set of journals which have thrown great light onto this time from a social, political and naval aspect but his real legacy lay in the naval reforms he set in place.

Samuel Pepys

Pepys first joined the admiralty as Clerk to the Acts of the Navy Board in 1654 under the patronage of his cousin, a naval officer Edward Montagu. In May 1660 he sailed to Holland with Montagu and brought back King Charles II taking personal responsibility for the king's beloved dog, a great honour despite the fact that in his diary he records that the spaniel *'shit the boat to the great amusement of us all'*. He committed himself totally to his employment and studied all aspects of his role and the running of a modern navy. He befriended the naval architect Anthony Deane and took an active role in the design of new warships and naval administration. He avoided being caught up in the fallout of the disastrous second Anglo-Dutch war due to his relationship with the king but quite simply the reasons for the disasters were lack of money and investment which was ultimately the responsibility of the crown and parliament.

Pepys is instrumental in having a vision of what a professional navy should be and it is this that makes him so important in the history of the Royal Navy and so vital to its evolution. He started the process of having professional career officers who knew their business as well as developing proper dockyards and standardising ship designs. In 1677 he set up standards for officers and steered through an act of parliament for thirty new warships including one of one hundred guns, two of ninety guns and twenty of seventy guns. The new system of leadership in the navy was to take on officers as midshipmen, then after three years promote them to lieutenant after an examination to be held in front of a board of senior officers, an oral examination still in use today in the Royal Navy. In 1684 he was made secretary to the Admiralty and headed a Royal Commission to restore warships. The making of a modern navy starts with Samuel Pepys and his role cannot be understated.

On the death of Charles II in 1665 the throne went to his brother James Duke of York. This in turn led to the Glorious Revolution of 1688 over fears of James leading England back into a Catholic state. Parliament turned to James's daughter Mary who had married William of Orange, King of the Netherlands and offered him the throne. William landed with an army at Torbay in 1688, significantly unopposed by the Royal Navy whose senior officers had indeed been a part of the approach made to William. James, unable to face such an army fled to Ireland and began plans to regain his throne with the help of Catholic France.

0n the 10th July 1690, an Anglo-Dutch fleet was engaged by a far superior French fleet off Beachy Head and tactically defeated. The Dutch lost nine ships and the Royal Navy one ship. The French lost no vessels. There were recriminations almost straight away, the English blamed the Dutch for engaging too soon and attacking the French line before reaching the beginning of it, in any event it caused the English fleet to run back through the Channel to the consternation of the spectators on shore. Panic ensued in England as fears of invasion became rampant. The army was with William in Ireland and should the French sail into the Irish sea this army could not be brought back to repel an invasion of England. As it happens the French did not exploit this tactical victory and sailed back to France to refit after the battle. The day after the battle William defeated James at the Battle of the Boyne thus removing the immediate possibility of James returning to England to retake the throne. The threat was finally removed in 1692 when the English and Dutch Navies defeated an attempted French invasion at the Battle of Barfleur. The aftermath of these battles saw Britain as the foremost naval power in Western Europe and probably the world. With such a close alliance it appears to have been decided that England should be the paramount naval power and that Holland relinquish her aspirations in favour of England who was better placed to exploit the situation.

Defeat at Beachy Head and victory at Barfleur was followed with financial disaster in June 1693 by the capture or destruction of ninety merchant ships bound for the Mediterranean at the first Battle of Lagos. This action was more significant than the defeat at Beachy Head in that it was termed the worst financial disaster since the Great Fire of London. The loss of half of the convoy was only a part of the calamitous effect of the Battle of Lagos. The convoy actually had two intentions, firstly to deliver the traders and their cargos into the Mediterranean and secondly to establish a permanent naval presence there, both of which failed. For me the loss of the trade fleet did as much for the Royal Navy as any victory ever did previously or since in that it caused the creation of a unique and valuable British asset, the Bank of England, and what was to become known, as the National Debt.

The loss of prestige after Beachy Head and the far more critical loss of money after Lagos caused the cry to go up from England, *'get the navy in shape'*. But how was this to be achieved? There was no money, the treasury was empty. In 1694 the Bank of England was founded with the sole object of collecting money from subscribers who would deposit the cash and in return receive an eight percent return on their investment, the National Debt as it has become known was born. Money raised was to be used on the navy and the return would come from the ability to trade overseas under the protection of the English flag and Royal Navy guns. Alongside this there is the boost given to industry at home in order to service the navy, ship building, cannon foundries, clothing and above all agriculture and farming, this was to lead eventually to the Royal Navy being the largest industrial organisation in the world. Throughout history the Royal Navy has led change through innovation and driven industrial and agrarian revolution starting with Henry VIII building his shipyards at Chatham within reach of the Royal Armoury at The Tower of London. At the end of the 17th century we see entrepreneurs in the north east combining coal mining and iron production to supply the navy with ordnance of all sizes. A book of the original subscribers to the Bank of England still exists in the vaults of the bank and top of this list are William and Mary themselves right the way down to common serving men and women.

The minimum investment was £25 and it is surprising to see how many subscribers were what one might consider ordinary people and low paid workers. £1.2 million was raised in less than two weeks of which half was spent on the navy. The investment did not stop there however. In 1704 a further £10,000 was invested in the navy in order to build facilities at Portsmouth and a further £40,000 for recruiting seamen, (among which were eight thousand Marines). Also, in 1704 Greenwich hospital was opened for the receipt of sick and injured sailors. In 1707 at the height of the War of the Spanish Succession a further £2.3m was raised for the Royal Navy. War has ever been a great mover in industrial and demographic change and this is as stark an example as one is ever likely to find.

The Race for Empire — 1700 to 1775

On the death of the childless Charles II of Spain in November 1700 the throne of Spain could potentially have gone to one of the two great dynasties of Europe at that time, Bourbon France or Habsburg Austria. France eventually won through with Philip of Anjou (grandson of Louis XIV) being crowned king. This led to war between France and a Grand Alliance led by The Holy Roman Empire and including Britain. The British parliament was split as to how to conduct this war with the Tories promoting a sea campaign of blockade and a war against trade and the Whigs claiming that a sea war could not win alone and that an army must be active on the continent. In the end both were used and both carried out their tasks successfully.

On 1st August 1704 British and Dutch Marines and sailors landed on the Gibraltar peninsular cutting off the Spanish garrison commanded by the governor Diego De Salinas who after four days' naval bombardment and siege, surrendered to Admiral Rooke. This has to be one of the most significant actions of the Royal Navy in British history and has shaped the British Empire ever since. Taking Gibraltar was difficult enough but holding it was another matter as on the 24th August a French fleet under the command of the Comte De Toulouse approached Gibraltar very likely with the intention of driving the Anglo Dutch fleet away and stranding the landing force on the rock where it would surely have withered and surrendered. Rooke forewarned of this venture sailed out and intercepted the French at what history has come to call the Battle of Malaga. The battle itself was inconclusive with neither side losing a ship, the Allied fleet suffering damage to rigging and spars and lacking ammunition after bombarding Gibraltar for several days, were unable to pursue the French and push home a decisive victory. The French retired on Toulouse and did not venture forth again, thus ceding the Western Mediterranean to the Allies and ultimately Britain who retained Gibraltar.

The Spanish War of Succession is best remembered in Britain for the exceptional campaigns and battles of John Churchill, the Duke of Marlborough. The capture and retention of Gibraltar cannot however be overestimated, one glance at a map of western Europe will show that Britain could now bottle up and control the two most vital points in western Europe, the English Channel and the Straits of Gibraltar. The great Duke carried out one of the greatest land campaigns in history and won several key battles but the capture of Gibraltar was a stunning strategic coup that was worth more than a hundred land victories at that time.

British strategic dominance was not to end there however as during the War of the Spanish Succession there were other prizes taken in North America which set Britain on a path of strategic dominance, Hudson Bay, Nova Scotia and Saint Christopher among them along with Menorca in the Balearic Islands. Britain's strategic pieces were now set for the wars that followed in the early to mid-18th century and would prove key to Britain's success in those wars

The first of these conflagrations, The War of Jenkins' Ear is remembered for its extraordinary title but is another episode in the continuing wars of the 18th century to gain control of rich trade routes and territories. Jenkins actually lost his ear in 1731 when it was removed by a Spanish captain but war was not declared until 1739 a full eight years later so I think that we can assume that the declaration of war was more to do with other considerations rather than as revenge for poor Captain Jenkins, however the severing of his ear did assist in stirring up aggression against Spain.

The real reasons for war are as outlined above, trade. With the Treaty of Utrecht after the War of the Spanish Succession Britain was granted an Asiento (trade agreement) to trade with Spanish colonies in the Caribbean and South America, mainly the sale of slaves. Britain passed this trading ability over to the South Sea Company who in 1739 along with various politicians spurred the British public into hostility with Spain, cynically using the Jenkins affair of eight years previously to stir up aggression in the hope of creating commercial gain. War was inevitable as it usually was in this bloody century and the Caribbean would be the battlefield.

One of the advocates of war with Spain was Admiral Edward Vernon who when an MP was a vigorous exponent of war with Spain and had recently taken over command of the fleet in the Caribbean, an experienced officer who had spent a great deal of his career in that area he knew of the significance of the ports of Portobello and Veracruz to Spanish trade. *'Old Grogum'* as he was known (a nickname after his old seagoing coat) decided on the outbreak of war to raid Portobello, with six sail of the line. The small force employed was calculated to diminish the chances of disease which so wracked most campaigns in that part of the world and the raid was successful in capturing the town in a day and leading to the destruction of port facilities and fortresses. However, despite the jubilation at home (the song Rule Britannia was composed to celebrate this event and a street would be named after Portobello in London) the raid did not have a major strategic effect. Vernon carried out various other raids mostly unsuccessful in the region, the main factor to failure being disease.

On the outbreak of war, a squadron was sent into the Pacific under Admiral George Anson to raid Spanish possessions and capture the Manilla treasure ship which he finally caught on the 20th June 1743 capturing an immense amount of silver both raw and pieces of eight. Anson then sailed home having circumnavigated the globe, a huge achievement. This and the raid on Portobello were the two most significant and positive results of the naval war for Britain. The War of Jenkins' Ear merged into the War of the Austrian Succession going from a primarily American war to Europe where Spain hoped to regain her possessions in Italy. The Spanish proved to be very competent at defending their possessions in the Caribbean and South America and as the war ended the relations between Britain and Spain improved significantly which proved to be of great value with Spain remaining neutral in the early years of the Seven Years War.

The Seven Years War has often been called the first true world war as it covered three continents and all the world's oceans and the Royal Navy was instrumental in Britain's military success, on the continent of North America especially. Britain's dominance in North America can be attributed to the army and land campaigns on a tactical basis but it was the Royal Navy who provided the strategic background for the victories on land by controlling the Atlantic Ocean and stopping the French from reinforcing their territories in New France. This strategic control was gained in 1759 with two of the most important battles in British history. These battles tend to be overlooked as Trafalgar has always been considered the biggest Royal Navy strategic victory in the age of sail but this chapter will show how the defeat of two French fleets would allow Britain to dominate the oceans and ultimately the new world and provide the ingredients for Britain's famous *'Annus Mirablis'* the year of wonder. The two battles are of Lagos and Quiberon Bay. I prefer to view these as part of the same overall picture and with this in mind I link them together for the purposes of this book and the reader will understand why as we progress through this narrative.

During 1759 the French devised a plan to invade England and Scotland by landing an army on the south coast and a follow up army in Scotland to incite rebellion against the Hanoverian monarchy. In order to achieve this an army was assembled near Vannes in Brittany and the French fleet at Toulon was ordered to sail to join the French fleet at Brest, link up and carry the army to England.

In May 1759 Admiral Boscawen was ordered to blockade Toulon whilst Admiral Sir Edward Hawke blockaded Brest. The First Sea Lord Admiral Anson had conceived the strategically inspired plan to sit the fleet to the NNW of Ushant. This allowed blockade of Brest (with an inshore squadron of frigates to observe and call in the main fleet in the event of a breakout) and to sit amid the trade route back to England covering any incoming convoys.

In late July 1759 Boscawen was forced back to Gibraltar with his fleet of fourteen sail of the line arriving on 4th August, to revictual and replace hands lost to action and disease. On 5th August, the French fleet of twelve sail of the line under Admiral La Clue left Toulon headed for Cadiz and then the mouth of the Loire to collect the army assembled at Vannes. On 17th August, the French fleet was spotted heading through the Straits of Gibraltar and Boscawen immediately gave chase in two divisions several hours apart. La Clue seeing this ordered his fleet to head out into the Atlantic for fear of being bottled up in Cadiz. However only half his fleet complied with this order, it is not known precisely why, either the following ships did not see the signal and the change in course in the diminishing daylight or the captains decided to continue to a friendly port. I know not which but bearing in mind there is always safety in numbers and with darkness fast approaching the chances of losing the British were high if the whole fleet continued out to sea together, I suspect it was the former reason of the two. In any event, the next morning La Clue hove to, to await the rest of his fleet, and saw eight sail of the line approaching which he mistook for the rest of his fleet, it was in fact the first division of Boscawen's fleet. The second division had been ordered to pursue the remainder of La Clue's fleet and blockade them in port.

The British very quickly overhauled La Clue and in the ensuing action captured the French ship *Centaure*, however in this initial action Boscawen's flagship *Namur* was badly damaged. That evening La Clue's fleet scattered with two ships escaping out to sea and the remaining four being pursued next day and bought to action off the coast. Two French ships were wrecked after being driven ashore and two more captured. Thus, the French Mediterranean fleet was neutralised and removed from the chess board in this most interesting war of empire.

After the battle of Lagos in August invasion of England was out of the question but the French military still harboured designs on an invasion of Scotland using the transports assembled in the Gulf of Morbihan, the ones assembled near Vannes being unable to put to sea without escort. Admiral Sir Edward Hawke continued his blockade NNW of Ushant until the first week of November when it was blown back to the Channel taking refuge in Torbay leaving a small squadron under Commodore Duff of five small sail of the line and nine frigates to watch the Gulf of Morbihan and the transports which were still rightly considered to be a threat.

As Hawke was forced back to Torbay and the gales subsided the French fleet under Admiral Conflans comprising twenty-one sail of the line and six frigates left Brest on the 14th November heading for the Gulf of Morbihan to collect the transports. On the 15th the fleet was spotted by a Royal Navy supply ship the *Love and Unity* seventy miles west of Belle Ille. This ship met with Hawke the following day, who had put back to sea after the gales, and passed on its vital intelligence to Hawke who set sail for Quiberon Bay hoping to intercept the French.

On the 19th Conflans was into Quiberon Bay and having spotted Duff's squadron gave chase. Duff scattered his fleet and headed out of the Bay to the NW with Conflans eagerly pursuing him when at eight thirty a.m. on the 20th Conflans spotted Hawke closing in from the north into the bay. Conflans then turned about and headed back into the bay and into a brisk gale believing that Hawke would not dare follow into those treacherous waters in such poor conditions. He was wrong, in the finest traditions of the Royal Navy Hawke pursued Conflans into the bay. An interesting decision on Hawke's part and one which owes a great deal to the trial and execution of Admiral Byng at the start of the Seven Years War, (Byng had been sent to reinforce Majorca but seeing the French fleet already besieging the island withdrew and was court-martialled for cowardice). Hawke believed that he could pursue and catch the French even at the expense of several ships foundering and not wishing to turn away and face the same consequences as Byng he swung into the bay and overtook the rear of the French line. At four p.m. the battered French ship of the line *Formidable* surrendered followed shortly after by the *Therese* and *Superbe*, the former foundering and the latter capsizing in the heavy seas. This was followed by the *Heros* which ran aground and surrendered before nightfall.

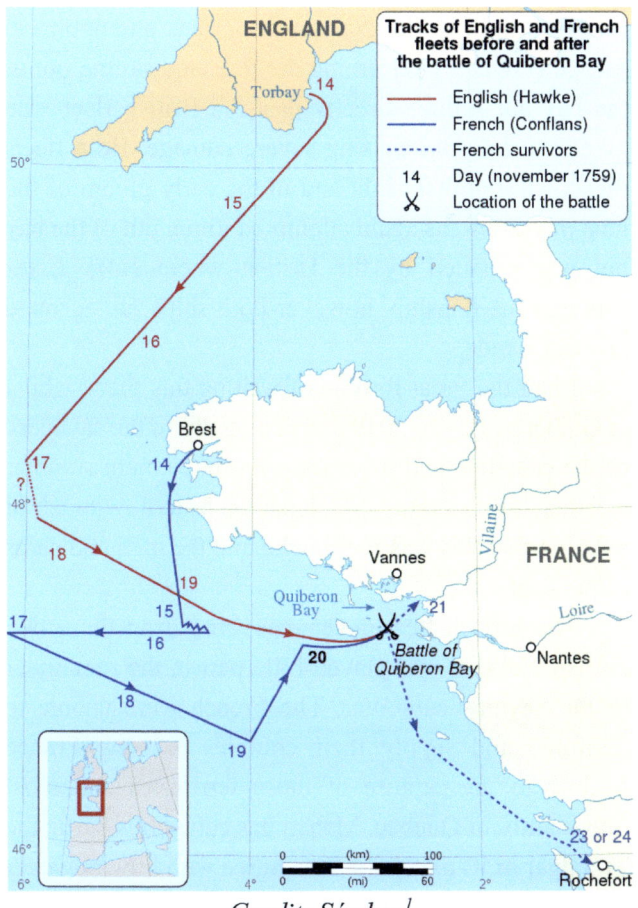

Credit: Sémhur[1]

---

[1] Published under Free Art License. Credit: Sémhur. Source: https://commons.wikimedia.org/wiki/File:Battle_of_Quiberon_Bay_-_1759_-_Tracks_map-en.svg

The night of the 20th saw Conflans attempting to escape Hawke by reforming the fleet and sailing out of the bay but sailing directly past the British fleet who raked the *Intrepid* causing severe damage. Both fleets then anchored that night and in the early gloom of the next day Conflans again attempted to run out of the bay but was pursued by the British where *HMS Essex* captured his flagship, however both ships ran aground on Four Sands.

I had the great fortune of writing this piece whilst at Quiberon Bay in 2019 and can testify to the savagery of the coastline and the tides, even in clement summer weather, so it cannot be understated as to how much of a daring feat this was for Hawke and the men and ships of his fleet.

The French fleet never recovered from these two British victories and played little part in the remainder of the Seven Years War. The French were unable to reinforce and supply their colonies in New France leading to the capture of those territories and most importantly of Quebec. Mahan has called this battle the Trafalgar of its day and I must agree with him, however as stated earlier I also include the earlier action of Lagos, which leads on to my final observation regarding the French economy

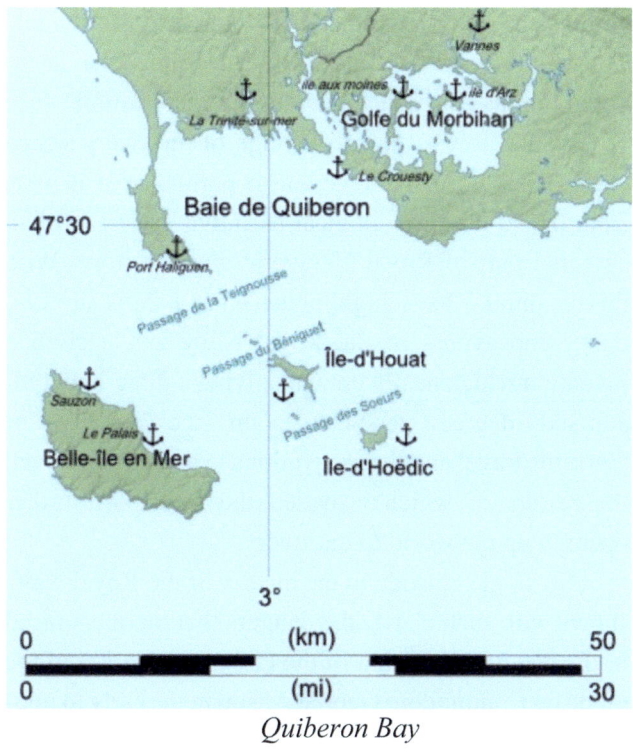

Quiberon Bay

Credit: GwenofGwened²

There were also the devastating financial consequences of these defeats. In short financiers lost faith in France's ability to operate against the Royal Navy and protect trade. We also see the loss of two

---

² Published under Creative Commons (https://creativecommons.org/licenses/by-sa/4.0/deed.en)
Source: https://en.wikipedia.org/wiki/File:C%C3%B4te_Sud_Morbihan_-_Baie_de_Quiberon.png

colonies in the Caribbean, Guadeloupe and Martinique. The result of this was the French Government having to default on its debt causing huge financial turmoil.

I want now to turn to the age of discovery which was always a difficult section to narrate as it departs from the so far chronological narrative but it is still an essential part of Royal Navy and world history. With this in mind I have highlighted what I think are two major endeavours of the Royal Navy and a civilian invention which neatly entwine giving a three-hundred-and-sixty-degree perspective on the dangers of maritime travel and the innovations to assist such travel, the results of which provided the means of further opening up the world to discovery.

No single episode in the history of the Royal Navy shows with such clarity the dangers that mariners faced in the age of sail as that of the circumnavigation of the globe by Commodore George Anson in the early to mid-1740s. This odyssey shows the extremes of all the enemies of seamen bar war itself, disease, inclement weather and general wear and tear on wooden ships of this period.

This extraordinary story starts on the 18th September 1740 when Anson sailed with a small squadron of six warships and two merchant ships, their orders were to round Cape Horn, sail up the coast of South America and capture the port of Callao which served the capital city of Peru, Lima. Thence on to Panama to lead a revolt of natives against their Spanish overlords and ultimately capture the Acapulco galleon. These very ambitious plans were most certainly driven by influential British merchants and with the resources available quite unachievable. The squadron was to embark five hundred soldiers to assist but these were not to be of the finest quality. Indeed, only about two hundred and fifty were made available and these were from the Royal Hospital at Chelsea, unfit and even sickly. The remainder of the force was to be made up with marines.

The squadron's first duty was to convoy a fleet of one hundred and fifty-two merchant ships from Britain and then sail to Portuguese Madeira. Spies had learnt of the venture (not uncommon bearing in mind how long it takes to assemble a squadron in port) and as a consequence a Spanish fleet was sent to intercept Anson's squadron off Madeira but failed to locate them. At Madeira the British squadron was able to transfer stores and return home one of the merchant ships. Conditions aboard the ships at this time were already horrendous as the ships overcrowded with stores and lying low in the water could not open the gun ports as was usual to assist with airflow in hot conditions. Thus began a two-month voyage to Isla de Santa Catarina in Brazil, two months where disease in the form of typhus and dysentery hit the unsanitary ships due to overcrowding. Typhus is spread by infected body lice and in the already confined ships (even more so with five hundred extra troops on board) spread rapidly. On reaching Isla De Santa Catarina a thorough cleaning of the ships was undertaken.

The most perilous part of the journey was now to be carried out, the rounding of Cape Horn. This was achieved by mid-March but in so doing two of the squadron were forced to return back into the Atlantic and finally to England. In the surviving ships however Scurvy, that scourge of the sailing mariner, broke out causing much weakness among the crews and the inability to carry out basic ship board functions. Unable to accurately calculate the longitude of the squadron the position was incorrectly thought to be three hundred miles west of the nearest land but this was proved incorrect when land was spotted only two miles off the starboard beam. The squadron hastily beat back out to sea and was subsequently scattered by a violent storm. The remaining ships then independently headed for the pre-arranged rendezvous point of Juan Fernandez. Here after several weeks the squadron reassembled minus the *Wager*, (see page 64) and minus two thirds of the original crews.

Whilst repairing ships at Juan Fernandez the *Centurion* sallied out and captured a small merchant ship which carried paperwork containing information that the Spanish squadron sent to intercept Anson at Madeira had failed to weather Cape Horn and returned back to the Atlantic, a decisive piece of information as this now left the entire Pacific open to Anson. The squadron set sail again heading north west for Paita in

Peru where it attacked and sacked the small port before heading for Acapulco to seize the galleon. Now down to just two ships, *Centurion* and *Gloucester*, (the others having been abandoned due to damage caused by the rounding of Cape Horn and the subsequent storm) Anson remained on station until early April waiting for the galleon, but had to withdraw to Mexico to water and realising he had missed the galleon decided to set sail and head west believing rightly that the galleon would sail for China rather than attempt Cape Horn with a British squadron in the area. Anson headed south to hit the trade winds but failed to find them as they had moved further south with the onset of summer and arrived at Macau on 11th November, having scuttled the *Gloucester* on route as it was literally falling apart.

Anson then took a huge gamble as a last ditched attempt to achieve something from the so far disastrous campaign by sailing to the Philippines to attempt to intercept the galleon, at last luck came Anson's way and on 20th June 1743, after a ninety-minute fight the Spanish galleon *Nuestra Senora De Cavadonge* was captured netting a massive haul of silver worth nearly $55m in today's money. Anson then set sail for home returning to England on the 11th July 1744 to a hero's welcome. Of the initial crews and soldiers that left England only one hundred and eighty-eight made it home aboard the *Centurion.*

The ultimately successful voyage of Anson was to increase the Royal Navy's global reach as it raised interest in the Pacific as a destination for commerce and conquest, a story taken up in the voyages of Captain Cook. This desire to expand into the Pacific also led to attempts to discover a north west passage to the Pacific through North America, a passage that eluded the world for many years.

Anson was to become one of the Royal Navy's most successful and influential admirals going on to victory over the French at the Battle of Cape Finisterre during the War of the Austrian Succession where he captured four ships of the line, two frigates and £300,000 in treasure. His experiences during the circumnavigation of the globe were to lead Anson to carry out major reforms when First Lord of the Admiralty during the Severn Years War. Among his reforms were the removal of corrupt defence contractors, improved medical care, submitting a revision of the Articles of War to tighten up discipline throughout the navy, uniforms for commissioned officers, the transfer of the marines from army to navy authority, and clarification of the system for rating ships according to their number of guns, 1st rates being the largest with over one hundred guns down to 6th rates of twenty-eight guns.

The war against the elements is just as important in the history of the Royal Navy as the great battles and campaigns which we know so well. We shall investigate in this section how the Royal Navy was to pioneer aids to navigation and lead the way to safe passage for all maritime traffic. Wrecks at sea are as old as time itself and even today we have dreadful examples of ships foundering in heavy seas, or simply because they are poorly maintained or sailed. One of the most serious losses of Royal Navy vessels took place on the 22nd October 1707. A fleet under the command of the respected and experienced Admiral Sir Cloudsley Shovel sailing up channel past the Scilly Isles crashed into the jagged rocks to the south of the islands losing four ships along with fifteen hundred men, including Admiral Shovel.

The basis for this terrible event was quite simply that navigational aids at that time could not calculate an exact position, or even a remotely confident position. Latitude could be calculated by the position of the sun and stars in relation to the equator and had been calculated thus for many years. However, longitude which was a fix east or west of a point of departure or known land position could not be accurately calculated, therefore a reliable fix could not be made on a land fall when crossing large oceans such as the Atlantic, Indian and Pacific. Thus Shovel, believing from dead reckoning that he was well west of the islands was in fact dangerously close.

Wrecks also had an impact on the day to day running of the Royal Navy and in particular in the discipline and morale of its sailors as at this time pay stopped when a seaman was no longer on board his ship, regardless of the reasons why. In 1741 there was the famous case of *HMS Wager*, a twenty-four gun former East India ship which formed part of Admiral Anson's squadron. She was wrecked off the coast of Chile in May of that year and as a consequence the crew refused to follow officers' orders and mutinied. When the survivors made it back to England and were court martialled for mutiny they quite simply insisted in their defence that as they no longer drew pay after the ship foundered, they were no longer subject to naval discipline. The Admiralty very wisely did not pursue the case but Anson realised the extreme danger of this existing system and as one of the Lords Commissioners in 1747 he was instrumental in applying an addition to the Mutiny Act of which the main purpose was:

'for extending the discipline of the navy to crews of His Majesty's ships, wrecked, lost or taken and continuing to receive wages upon certain conditions'.

This act neatly cleared that very dangerous loophole in the system and greatly enhanced discipline and morale amongst seamen as they were now paid despite the loss of their ship. Interestingly this did not extend to the merchant service and up to 1941 merchant seamen adrift after the loss of their ship were not paid.

This act was of great help in maintaining order on naval ships but it failed to stop the rather disagreeable practice of people in coastal regions either taking advantage of shipwrecks or deliberately inducing a wreck in order to plunder the cargo. There are no records of anybody ever being prosecuted for this crime which was classed as one of the crimes of *'The Bloody Code'* but there is much contemporary evidence to suggest that this practice was not merely myth. In 1753 a Wrecks Act was passed with the penalty of death for inciting a shipwreck or deliberately causing a ship to founder.

These changes were important in making provision for sailors but there still remained the problem of fixing longitude. In 1714 the government passed the Longitude Act which promised prize money of £20,000 to anybody who could arrive at a solution for calculating longitude.

This challenge was taken up by a remarkable and exceptionally clever carpenter and clock maker called John Harrison who in 1730 begun his experiments in the creation of the Maritime Chronometer. Not an easy task when one has to consider the extreme challenges that such a chronometer has to cope with. To begin with you have corrosion from the salty sea and air, then there are the changes in air pressure, humidity and temperature in different climates and weather patterns. Lastly there is the need to compensate for the often-violent movement of a ship at sea.

The end chronometer named the H5 was the product of over thirty years of work by John Harrison. This timepiece proved to be incredibly accurate and a copy, the K1, was used by James Cook on his second and third voyages. Now thanks to Harrison ships could make accurate landfall by successfully plotting the latitude by means of the sun and longitude by means of Harrison's chronometer. The seas of the world were open to the Royal Navy and a fledgling empire was thus nurtured and allowed to grow.

No informed study of the Royal Navy's scientific endeavours would be complete without the exploits of that great navigator James Cook. As an expert navigator he paved the way for exploration and discovery. Joining the Merchant Navy in 1755 Cook helped to successfully navigate the mouth of the St Lawrence River which was essential to the successful capture of Quebec. This brought him to the attention of both the Royal Society and the Admiralty. During the 1760s Cook's skills were put to the test in mapping Newfoundland while serving in *HMS Grenville*. Cook also conducted an observation of the solar eclipse of 1766. By obtaining an accurate estimate of the start time and finish of the eclipse and then comparing these to timings at a point in England he was able to calculate the longitude of the observation point in Newfoundland.

Cook's work in Newfoundland produced the first large scale accurate maps of the coastline and the first hydrographic surveys (shorelines, tides, currents and seabed) to use precise triangulation in order to establish accurate coastlines, these maps are still in use today.

In 1768 Cook was commissioned and given command of the Barque *Endeavour* in order to carry out a scientific expedition into the Pacific where it was intended to record the transit of Venus across the sun, thus hopefully providing an accurate distance of the earth from the sun, however this was not as accurate as was hoped for and Cook then went on to try and locate Terra Australis, a large continent that was believed to exist in the south seas. He started by sailing the *Endeavour* to New Zealand through the islands of Polynesia, the first European to do so, creating maps as he went. From New Zealand he sailed west and arrived at the east coast of the Australian continent on 19th April 1770, he landed at what he later named Botany Bay and subsequently claimed the land for King George. Unbeknownst to Cook at the time the coast of Australia had already been sighted by the French explorer Louis De Bouganville, however Bouganville could not find a way through the Great Barrier Reef so continued on his way. How different the world would be had he landed and claimed possession for France, no other part of the then empire and the current Commonwealth can be closer to England than Australia. Sadly, Cook was to meet his death in Hawaii when he was killed by natives who were attempting to steal one of his ships boats. Captain Cook's great voyages of discovery and his superb cartography and navigation of the as yet uncharted oceans and lands not only expanded the empire but also provided maps which due to their accuracy are still in use today by all nations.

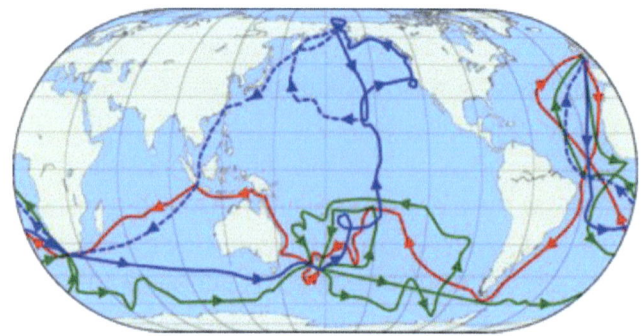

Cook's three voyages
Credit: Jon Platek [3]

---

[3] Published under Creative Commons (https://creativecommons.org/licenses/by-sa/3.0/deed.en) Source:
https://en.wikipedia.org/wiki/File:Cook_Three_Voyages_59.png

Revolution and Liberation — 1775 to 1815

We now come to the most glorious and romantic period in Royal Navy history, the golden age of sail. The period between the end of the Seven Years War and the ending of the French and Napoleonic Wars in 1815 was to see the Royal Navy secure itself as the paramount naval force on the globe jealously guarding a rich and prosperous commercial empire which would become the envy of the world. In this period, we see tragedy and triumph in equal measure with the loss of the American colonies but also the victory of the Battle of the Saintes which saved the West Indies colonies which in terms of trade were far more important than the thirteen colonies which clung on to the fringes of eastern America. We see technological development that allowed the Royal Navy to win this decisive victory in the West Indies which in turn led ultimately to the fall of the monarchy in France.

As we have seen with the exploits of Captain Cook in the previous chapter even in peace-time the Royal Navy was not idle, she had defence of the empire to carry out as well as expansion through exploration but as always in this turbulent period war was never far away and Britain's victories in the Seven Years War against France had caused huge resentment and a thirst for revenge in the French and in particular their king, Louis XVI. The period after the Seven Years War saw a huge and alarming expansion of the French fleet with the rebuilding of dockyards and ultimately a fleet of over eighty warships. A fleet with but one purpose, destruction of the Royal Navy and the establishment of France as the primary land and sea power in the world, all Louis needed was an opportunity to strike and this came from three thousand miles away in the Americas, The American Revolutionary War. But what of the Royal Navy at this time? Victory in war pays many dividends but after a world war when your main enemy has been humbled and virtually bankrupted it is common to seek the peace dividend of cost reductions in armed forces and the Royal Navy was certainly a victim of this. There were plenty of frigates and smaller vessels to patrol the empire but the battlefleet was to a large extent mothballed. One admiral complained that of his fleet of thirty-eight ships only nine were seaworthy. At the outbreak of war in the colonies of America, the British army on the continent was locked into a series of selected fortified positions which could only be supplied by sea. To this end the Royal Navy was to escort in convoy merchant ships to and from America to guard against American privateers who were very successfully praying on merchant ships. The army was very reliant on this resupply from across the Atlantic, every biscuit and bullet had to come from Britain. France now seized her chance and sided with the rebels in America by declaring war on Britain in 1778 followed by Spain and The Netherlands shortly after. Since the end of the Seven Years War the world had shifted now from France, the nation to be most concerned about to Britain. Until the end of the Seven Years War Britain had stood with other nations against the primary power in Europe, France, now due to her gains in the war she found herself in that position and of course outnumbered. Matters were to come to a head in 1781 when the French fleet under Admiral Comte De Grasse arrived off Chesapeake Bay where a British army was under siege at Yorktown. The British fleet off the coast attempted to intercept the French at the Battle of Chesapeake Bay but was unsuccessful in turning it away and the French troops which were transported to join Washington were instrumental in the ultimate surrender of the British Army at Yorktown. The killer blow however had been the failure of Admiral Grave's fleet to dislodge the French fleet from Chesapeake Bay and the inability to supply the army. The Revolutionary War was over and America lost due to an almost non-event in terms of a naval battle but it was to lead to a far greater danger, the vulnerability of the West Indies.

The loss of the colonies was a bitter blow to Britain but they were still second in importance to the West Indies, the home of British prosperity. George III realised the importance of the islands and summed up the situation by declaring: *'The West Indies must be defended, even at the risk of invasion of England'*. Loss of these important islands would have devastated the British economy and very likely stopped the empire in its tracks. A quarter of all imports to Britain (sugar) came from the West Indies, about £3m at that time and whole trading cities such as Liverpool and Glasgow relied on the carrying of that commodity across the Atlantic.

We now look at the technical innovations which would ultimately save the islands and the empire by considering a little known figure in Royal Naval history, The Navy Controller at that time Charles Middleton (later Lord Barham and First Lord of the Admiralty). For my money equally as important as Pepys for his administrative skills and industry but also for bringing to the Royal Navy the innovative upgrading of coppering and sheathing to British warships. All wooden vessels are subject to two great enemies at sea, ship worm and weed. Ship worm burrow deep into wooden hulls and eat their way through causing tremendous damage and weakening the frames of ships. Weed connects itself to wooden hulls and growing further slows down a ship's speed and lessens its manoeuvrability. This means that ships have to return to dry dock periodically especially when operating in tropical climates where the effects of worm and weed are far more virulent. There were no dry docks in the West Indies and now that America was gone the problem arose of how to keep a fleet at sea without a dry dock facility. The answer was coppering the bottom of warships. A ship builder in the north west of England had contacted Middleton with a suggestion of coppering war ships, as he had done for merchant ships sailing in African waters, a tried and tested method. Middleton was convinced of the need to carry out this upgrade and with the First Lord of the Admiralty Lord Sandwich he approached King George III directly with a scale model of a copper-bottomed ship and in turn convinced the king of the need to coat ships with this protective undercover. With the king's backing the Royal Navy went ahead coppering as many ships as possible and by 1782 the West Indies Squadron under Admiral Rodney was ready for action with this new technological advantage. To quote one Royal Navy captain of its effects:

'The advantages from the helm alone is immense, as they feel them instantly, and wear in one third of the distance they ever did...'

Alongside this we see the invention of a new piece of ordnance for the Royal Navy. Visitors to *HMS Victory* at Portsmouth dockyard will have noticed on the top deck close to the front of the ship two squat cannon vastly different from the other guns on board. These are Carronades. Named after the Carron Iron Foundry in Scotland where they were first designed and manufactured these are basically giant shotguns for close-in fighting. They fired a massive thirty-two-pound shot which would sweep the decks of enemy ships taking dozens of men with them. This decisive weapon was soon replacing the smaller guns on top decks of warships and were carried in over half of Rodney's fleet. The increase in speed provided by coppering and the introduction of the carronade were to prove decisive in what I think was a battle of just as much importance in this era as Trafalgar, the Battle of the Saintes in 1782.

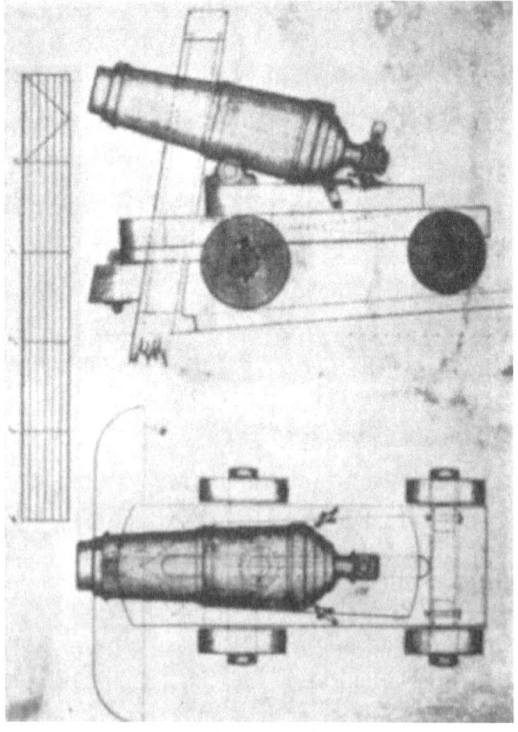

Corronade

On 7th April 1782 the French Admiral Comte De Grasse left Martinique with thirty-five sail of the line and an invasion force of fifteen thousand troops heading for Jamaica. The fleet was accompanied by merchant ships ready to offload on the captured island, a sign of French confidence which had been bolstered by the defeat of the British at Yorktown and the seeing off of the British fleet under Admiral Graves at Chesapeake Bay. De Grasse believed that the West Indies were open to invasion and capture and a severe blow could be dealt to the British by seizing such a prize. Hearing news of the French departure the British fleet under Admiral Rodney left St Lucia on the 8th April in hot pursuit of De Grasse with the intention of engaging and destroying the fleet and scuppering any chance of invasion. On the 9th Rodney caught up with the French who were astonished at the speed of the British ships due to the coppering, to quote one French captain during the subsequent action, *'The French ships were like tortoises chasing British stags'*. The British vanguard under Admiral Hood soon caught up with the rear of the French fleet causing much damage to the French ships and forcing De Grasse to withdraw to a safer distance and on the 10th April De Grasse withdrew still further away from the British, still intent on carrying out the invasion of Jamaica. It was at this time that two French ships *Zele* and *Magnanime* collided with each other and Rodney decided to close with them hoping that De Grasse would turn to protect them, which he did. This brought the fleets closer together and the prospects of a major engagement became more likely, especially with the speed of the British ships. On 12th April Rodney finally caught up with the French and after the wind had shifted, he used his squadrons to split the line, a forerunner of the tactic used so decisively by Nelson twenty-three years later but without the all-encompassing destruction that Trafalgar delivered.

Credit: ChristiaandeWet[4]

The breaking of the line brought into play that other great invention spoken of earlier, the carronade. Passing

---

[4] Published under GNU license
(https://commons.wikimedia.org/wiki/Commons:GNU_Free_Documentation_License,_version_1.2). Source:
https://commons.wikimedia.org/wiki/File:Battle_of_the_Saintes_plan.jpg

between ships the British were able to sweep the decks from stem to stern causing huge losses on the French warships overcrowded with troops for the invasion of Jamaica. By breaking the line, the British fleet was now between the French and their objective forcing De Grasse to withdraw the shattered fleet in small groups to the south west pursued by the British fleet who caught several French ships and captured De Grasse himself.

The French Admiral De Grasse, a very capable man, had been taken and his fleet shattered along with nine thousand dead and wounded and over half his invasion army captured. In total seven French ships had been destroyed or captured during the battle and the days following. The Saintes was a decisive victory for Rodney and the Royal Navy. It had saved Jamaica and the West Indies and therefore saved the empire and Britain itself. Despite the huge amounts of money poured into the French Navy the Royal Navy was still dominant and the French monarchy was now in serious danger, having spent so much with no return the cost to the nation was enormous and the consequent economic backlash would lead eventually to revolution and another war.

On a blustery day in 1771 a young boy of twelve years old was rowed across the Medway to join a warship and start a naval career that would make him both famous and inspirational for centuries to come.

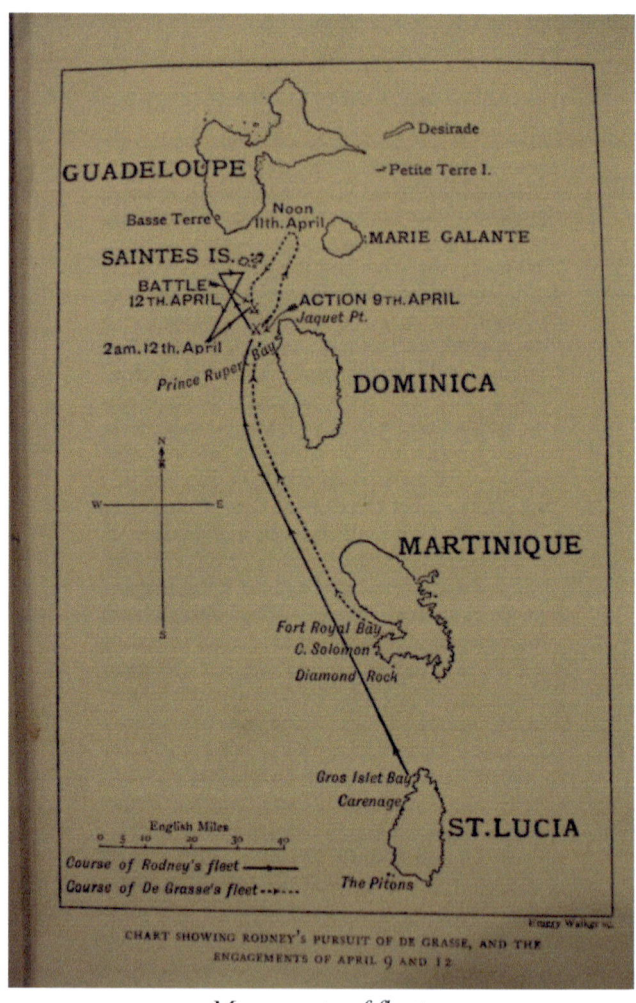

Movements of fleets

He was joining the ship as a midshipman at a time when the Royal Navy was in between wars but almost at the pinnacle of its greatness, a pinnacle the young boy would help the navy attain in the coming years. His name was Horatio Nelson and as he passed the great ships of the line at anchor, he perhaps stared in wonder at the massive three deck line of battleship *HMS Victory,* the ship that would ultimately bare him to fame and glory in one of the greatest and most decisive sea battles in history, Trafalgar.

HMS Victory

The road to this victory would be long and fraught and would see Britain close to invasion from the old enemy France but ultimately see her victorious along with her Allies in saving Europe from a tyrannical dictator. The story starts long before Napoleon and traces back to 1792 and revolution in France.

The destruction of the French fleet and the hopes of the nation were dashed at The Saintes in 1782 and with it the vast expenditure on the navy which France could ill afford. The result of this and other pressing issues in France led to revolution in 1792 and the beheading of the king and queen a year later. At first Britain was not concerned by these events, they were continental and if France was in turmoil so much the better for Britain. But events soon overtook them when the new French Republic declared war in 1793 ranging herself against almost every power in Europe. This was a most desperate series of wars for Britain which threatened her very survival and way of life. French republicanism threatened the very existence of the British monarchy and victory for France would have put Britain and Europe into the hands of a tyrannical system of government that would have shaped the world for years to come. Once again and not for the last time the Royal Navy would be at the forefront of this battle protecting Britain and her interests with those famed wooden walls.

As outlined above for Britain this would primarily be a naval war. Armies were eventually used both in

Spain and France to great success culminating in victory at Waterloo in 1815 but it was the policy of Britain to prefer to provide money to European states to fight on land leaving the sea to the Royal Navy which allowed protection of the all-important trading empire. At the end of these wars, we see Britain as the leading naval power in the world and what one may well term today as a superpower, the only one of its time. The Royal Navy after 1815 would reign supreme for nearly a hundred years creating that great period in British and world history, the *Pax Britannica*. This supremacy would come at a price however not least of all in the way the navy functioned with the common seaman becoming more prominent and the often-harsh conditions of life at sea coming to a head with the joint mutinies of Spithead and the Nore and the Admiralty and national response.

How was this new challenge met by the Royal Navy in 1793 and what were the first duties of this fighting force? The French fleet or what was left of it was in a sorry state after the revolution, many officers being removed and even executed and ships laid up in port with insufficient crews. From the outset the French republic was assailed by her land enemies first and foremost whilst Britain carried out her usual blockade and convoy duties. There were what I think six major engagements at sea in this period which had a direct influence on the outcome of the wars, The Glorious First of June, Cape St Vincent, Camperdown, The Nile,

Copenhagen and Trafalgar. I want to look at these battles and explore their effect on the outcome of the wars so let us look at the first of these, The Glorious First of June.

As described earlier the French Navy was for the most part in port, laid up and without the essential supplies to put to sea. The navy was needed though very early on in the war as a convoy escort for a huge grain fleet. In 1793 the harvest in France failed causing the very real possibility of a famine. Therefore, the French Government turned to her old ally the United States and purchased several thousand tons of grain which needed to be shipped back to France. In Spring 1794 a vast convoy of one hundred and twenty-five merchant ships set off from the United States bound for France carrying the much needed cargo whilst a fleet of twenty-six sail of the line under Admiral Villaret De Joyeuse was sent from Brest to meet the convoy and escort it to French ports. In Britain Admiral Howe was dispatched with twenty sail of the line and fifteen frigates to intercept the convoy finally making contact with the French battle fleet on the 28th May four hundred miles west of Ushant. Howe after a lengthy chase engaged the French fleet but evening was approaching and the battle soon petered out after one French and one British ship had been severely damaged and forced to retire.

The next morning Howe again engaged ordering the fleet to break the French line and bring on a general melee, however many captains did not see the order due to the smoke and a breaking of the line was not achieved. On the subsequent two days that bane of sea travel, fog, descended and the fleets lost sight of each other until the 1st June when the fog cleared and Howe again sighted Villaret De Joyeuse and engaged the French in line of battle. Once again Howe ordered the fleet to break the line and this was done so with far greater success than the previous day and in under an hour the French ships were beginning to break away and scatter. Howe signalled general chase but nineteen of the French ships got away after Villaret De Joyeuse managed to reform them. Six French ships were captured and eleven British ships badly damaged, mainly in the rigging, two of which were dismasted entirely. The losses and damages of each fleet highlight very starkly the difference in tactics employed by the French and the British at this time. The British would pound away at a ship's hull preparatory to boarding whereas the French would aim for the rigging and attempt to cripple British ships. To me this clearly indicates the aggressive nature of the Royal Navy at this time, close in, grapple and board and take the fight to the enemy. The French tactics show far more caution and reluctance in grappling with the British at close quarters. There is no suggestion here of a reluctance to fight on the part of the French, simply an appreciation of the period and a French understanding that her ships and men were not in any condition to come to close grips with the Royal Navy. As noted earlier the French fleet was stagnating in port, undermanned and lacking the discipline of constant sea duty which the British enjoyed. Life at sea in the age of sail for the Royal Navy consisted of tedious months at sea beating back and forth outside French ports or on convoy duty, constantly altering sail in all weathers. This created a tough disciplined seaman who followed orders and conducted sail drill and gunnery with an almost industrial rhythm. The French fleet and crews could never hope to match this expertise and aggression, especially with most of the officer corps having been removed in the revolution.

Was the Glorious First of June a Royal Navy victory? Interesting question and I have to say yes and no. No because the grain convoy was not intercepted and successfully reached France. That grain proved decisive in allowing France to continue the war. Had it not arrived and a famine ensued a further revolution may well have occurred and possibly the monarchy restored. It was of course a Royal Navy tactical victory, the first of the war and decisive in that six enemy ships were taken, a good tally for any battle in those days of sail. The newly envisaged tactic of breaking the enemy line had been vindicated and set the scene for future battles at sea. It proved that the Royal Navy had maintained the skill and daring of the Seven Years War and the Battle of The Saintes and that unless the French carried out major reform of their navy the seas would forever be British and the ability to carry the fight to Britain most unlikely.

We now move forward two years to the eventful year of 1796. In August of that year Spain declared war on Britain allying herself with France, a customary alliance not unexpected at the time, and bringing with it the Spanish Navy which was a formidable force. The consequence of Spain's entry into the war forced the Royal Navy Mediterranean fleet under Sir John Jervis to quit the bases at Corsica and Elba and move to Gibraltar where the fleet could bottle up Spanish and French ships in the Mediterranean and operate in the Atlantic covering the coasts of France and Spain. One of the fleet's duties was to blockade the Spanish fleet at Cadiz and if they ventured out to engage and destroy them. On 14th February 1797 one of the scouting frigates of Jervis's inshore squadron watching Cadiz reported that the Spanish fleet was out and approaching the British fleet just off Cape St Vincent. Jervis's Mediterranean fleet had fifteen sail of the line, including the newly arrived seventy-four gun *HMS Captain* the flagship of Commodore Horatio Nelson. Over the horizon the Spanish fleet was seen approaching numbering twenty-seven sail of the line including the Spanish Admiral Jose De Cordoba's huge flagship *Santissima Trinidad* of one hundred and thirty-two guns, the largest warship afloat.

The Spanish fleet not only outnumbered the British fleet it also outgunned it by 2308 cannon to 1232. However, the aggressive spirit of the Royal Navy again came to the fore with Jervis ignoring the numerical superiority of the Spanish. As the Spanish ships were being counted Jervis stopped the count saying, *'were there fifty ships I would still engage them'*. Not just bravado, the Spanish though numerically superior were not of the quality of the Royal Navy. Like the French they had been blockaded in port for months and lacked crews and experience, in addition to this they were approaching in open order, widely separated in two groups and not in battle formation. Jervis decided to take advantage of this by splitting his force into two columns and sailing between the two Spanish groups, subsequently engaging the group to port. However, this allowed Cordoba heading the other group to starboard of Jervis to head away on an opposite course and thus avoid battle. This is where Nelson was to show his initiative as he could see from the deck of the *Captain*, that the Spanish were getting away. Despite orders to the contrary, he broke off from the main line and headed to engage the lead ship of the Spanish line and thus slow the group down enabling Jervis to catch up. It worked perfectly but Nelson soon found himself engaging and grappling the *San Nicholas* a Spanish seventy-four gun ship. Nelson personally led a boarding party and captured the ship only to find that another 74 the *San Josef* was alongside the *San Nicholas* threatening to board and recapture her. This is where Nelson showed his courage and tenacity by again leading a boarding party from the *San Nicholas* onto the *San Josef* with the cry, *'Westminster Abbey or glorious victory'*. This aggressive and daring attack was to lead to the capture of both ships, an extraordinary feat. Cordoba retired with the remains of his fleet back to Cadiz having lost four ships captured and three that would never fight again. Jervis on hearing of Nelson's initiative personally thanked him despite the fact that Nelson had disobeyed orders. This did raise some eyebrows among several of Jervis's other officers but he defended Nelson by stating that if any other of his officers behaved in the same way with the same results, he would be equally grateful. The traditional fighting instructions were proving too rigid for Nelson, he was convinced that flexibility was the key to success and a level of independence required for ships' captains to follow their instincts.

The Battle of Cape St Vincent was a great and welcome victory for the Royal Navy. Fifteen British ships had defeated a Spanish fleet of twenty-seven and forced them back into port at Cadiz. The Spanish ships had a greater number of guns and men but the highly trained and disciplined men of the Royal Navy were able to soundly beat this inexperienced Spanish fleet. The Spanish men fought fiercely but without direction, it is clear that Cordoba had not intended to engage the British fleet, simply to sail past it and link up with a French fleet further up the coast.

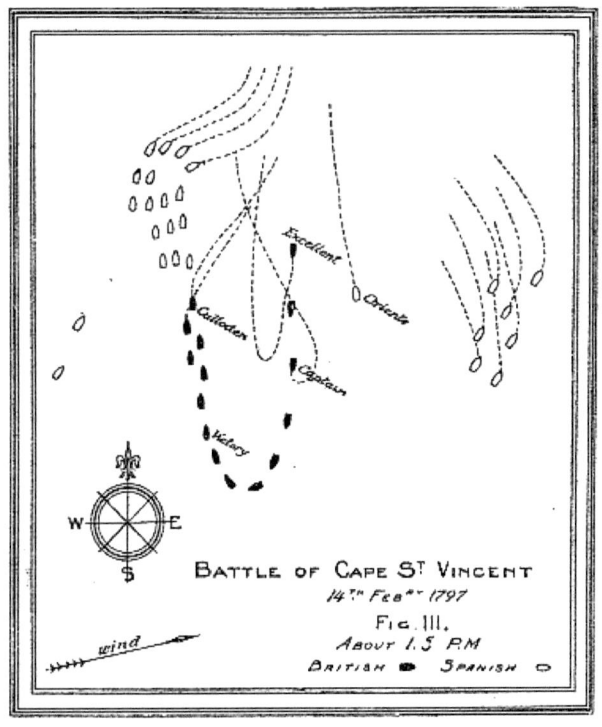

Events now moved to the North Sea and home waters where Britain's old and gracious enemy the Dutch had allied with France. The Dutch fleet was as formidable as one hundred and fifty years before and the men excellent seamen of great courage and experience. Blockading them in port was the job of Admiral Duncan and the North Sea Fleet but trouble was brewing closer to home for the Royal Navy in the form of mutiny in the fleet.

Within the space of a few years the Royal Navy had grown to over one thousand ships and manpower had increased from a peacetime total of around sixteen thousand to over one hundred and twenty thousand. Unfortunately, with this increase came dissatisfaction among the ranks of ordinary seamen and these grievances were to come to a head with two large scale mutinies.

In April 1797 seamen of the Channel fleet at Spithead (just off Portsmouth) decided to join together and petition the Admiralty with a list of grievances. Top most of these was pay. Wages had not changed since the time of Cromwell yet with the advent of war inflation had steadily risen and it was becoming almost impossible for seamen to provide for their families ashore. In the eyes of the seamen, they were the backbone of the navy and the defenders of the country yet were neglected by the government and society. They were not alone in this of course, the regular soldiers of the army felt much the same and were treated just as poorly regarding wages. This sadly was not to change for the army until the Great War, unfortunately throughout history and especially in the period up to World War I the nation has shown a great lack of concern with its fighting men. Sailors and soldiers crippled by action often became beggars. Alongside the issue of wages there was also the discontent of the so called 'purser's pound' a form of corruption where the pound of weight was equal to fourteen ounces as opposed to the regular sixteen ounces, the difference going to the purser. The victualing of ships by the purser system was ever controversial and many unscrupulous pursers had successfully lined their pockets at the expense of the sea going navy. Ships at sea would often open casks of meat only to find that the top layer was of acceptable quality yet the remainder of the cask was full of rotten meat. The purser's pound was a clear and open fiddle which had become accepted but loathed and resented by the seamen. On top of this there was the ever-growing cruelty of officers towards seamen. This is probably due to the expansion of the navy in wartime where experienced officers had to be supplemented by inexperienced privileged gentlemen who carried the aristocratic principle to the decks of ships often with tragic results. Indeed in 1797 the crew of the Frigate *Hermione* mutinied in the West Indies murdering all the officers after the strict captain Hugh Pigot had ordered that the last man down from the rigging would be flogged. As a result, two men fell to their deaths leading to the mutiny.

The petition was presented to the Admiralty by the mutineers at Spithead describing *'the many hardships and oppressions we have laboured under for many years, which, we hope, your lordships will address as soon as possible'*. This was particularly aimed at the low wages and the petition went on to say *'that we might be the better able to support our wives and families in a manner comfortable'*. These were not unreasonable demands and throughout the mutiny the seamen always said that if the French came out they would sail out to meet them and fight, no officers were hurt and the whole thing was rather amicable. The Admiralty and government were concerned by the mutiny however as it was akin to the revolution in France which frightened the ruling classes so wages were raised, many of the concessions were met and the whole thing hushed up. The war with France was becoming an extreme drain on the economy and the increase in sailors' wages along with the growing expense of shipbuilding and maintaining allies abroad put a huge strain on the treasury. In 1799 in order to support the tax system already in place the government introduced income tax with anyone earning over £60 a year being liable to pay. This was a huge change in policy and much criticised at the time. Tax had always been in existence of course with land tax being the main source supplemented by taxes on what were deemed as luxury items such as servants, carriages, ribbons and bizarrely windows but the revenue was not enough and credit was at its limit. This highly controversial move was expected to only last a short time (the duration of the war) then be repealed and the act ripped up and destroyed, alas it still remains to this day.

A word or two should be said here of the system of press ganging. The romantic image of the navy at this time is of squads of seamen roaming ashore dragging men out of their homes and workplaces to fill the manpower shortage of the fleet. Certainly, this did happen, but only in times of desperation and extreme national emergency, it was not a practice carried out often. For its part the navy wanted experienced sailors, therefore most press ganging was carried out at sea with men taken from merchant ships, often foreign, indeed it was extreme press gang activity that contributed to the war of 1812 with the United States. Landsmen as they were called were taken but this was mainly through the scouring of the prisons as an alternative to incarceration or deportation and some volunteers.

Romanticised image of a press gang

It has to be remembered that a life at sea was certainly no harsher than life on land and in some ways better. Most crimes committed on land carried the sentence of death or deportation whereas the vast majority of crimes at sea were covered by flogging. There were three square meals a day on board ship (square meal comes from the wooden plates used on ship which were square shaped) with ingredients no worse than those found on land, indeed somewhat better as they contained far more meat. The calorie intake of a seaman was around five thousand calories a day and had to be due to the strength and endurance needed to sail a ship. That great scholar of the 19th century Dr Johnson did comment that no man would choose going to sea, if he could contrive to get himself into prison but I think that is far off the mark. Along with the benefits described above there was also the prospect of action and prize money and many common sailors returned home wealthy in their own right.

Despite the cover up of events at Spithead news of the mutiny did spread to the fleet at the Nore and a further mutiny occurred with more concessions demanded. This time the Admiralty stood firm and refused to victual the ships thus starving the seamen into submission. There were four hundred arrests for mutiny and twenty-nine executions but the mutiny was suppressed allowing the North Sea fleet to sail out in October 1797 to confront that old respected adversary the Dutch.

The Dutch now under the name of the Batavian Republic were allied to France and constituted a direct threat to Britain in home waters, therefore the North Sea fleet under Admiral Duncan was set to watch the Dutch and blockade the fleet in harbour. In October 1797 the Dutch fleet numbering eleven sail of the line and frigates sailed from the Texel with the intention of linking up with a French fleet preparing to invade Ireland. The Dutch under Admiral De Wynter were soon intercepted by the North Sea fleet and despite the danger of shallows Admiral Duncan led his force into the attack off Camperdown. Similar to the Battle of Cape St Vincent the British formed two lines with the intention of splitting the Dutch fleet. This was first achieved by the line under Admiral Onslow attacking the rear of the Dutch line and very soon four Dutch ships were encircled and subsequently overwhelmed. The van of the Dutch line was then engaged by Duncan and after a severe pounding De Wynter struck his colours and surrendered.

Eleven ships were taken and the threat in home waters to the north was for the time being diminished, events now turned to the Mediterranean again with the Royal Navy re-entering the region in strength.

As we have seen in the previous three battles in this chapter and the Battle of the Saintes the splitting of an enemy line of battle could be a major battle winning tactic and one admiral in particular would hone this tactic and use it to its fullest effect, that man was Admiral Nelson. The whole purpose of a line of battle was to ensure ships discipline and the ability to bring the maximum firepower to bear on the enemy. There were disadvantages of course such as having to endure the same punishing broadsides in return but the Royal Navy's mastery of faster loading would in the age of sail provide the difference with often three rounds being fired to every one of the enemies. The biggest disadvantage though in my mind is that the lead ships of the line which contained the commanders could not always see what was happening behind them and the rigid code of the fighting instructions meant that captains could not work on their own initiative as Nelson had done at Cape St Vincent. Battles were won with the line of battle tactic but there were few crushing defeats, the French or Spanish would limp home to port but would still constitute a threat and force the Royal Navy to blockade. A more destructive method was needed to destroy fleets and remove the threat for good and Nelson saw the splitting of the line as the answer. Not strictly a Nelsonian idea, splitting the line had been advocated some years before by a Scottish theoretical tactician John Clerk who approached the Admiralty with a tactic of attacking from 'to windward' and cutting the line, a tactic used to great effect at The Saintes and Camperdown. Nelson was an avid reader of Clerk's theories and endeavoured to put them into practice in a practical way in order to achieve a decisive victory at sea. Nelson instructed his captains to study Clerk's work and often quoted from the ideas, he clearly saw the benefits.

Having withdrawn from the Mediterranean in 1796 the Royal Navy was sent back in on a mission to discover what the French were up to in that region as intelligence had been gathered regarding a build-up of land and sea units at Toulon. Admiral Nelson with a small squadron was dispatched to investigate but was unable to ascertain much so after receiving ten ships of the line as reinforcements Nelson headed for Toulon to blockade the port only to find that Bonaparte had departed along with thirty thousand men and a dozen ships of the line. Assuming correctly that the French were headed for Egypt to open a land route to India Nelson pursued them and after much searching found them at Alexandria. The army had already landed but without supplies could not last long so Nelson decided to attack the French fleet at anchor in Aboukir Bay. Nelson always allowed independent thought and action from his subordinates and it was Captain Thomas Foley of the *Goliath* who spotted that though the French were aligned in a defensive crescent formation there was room to go between the lead ship and the shore and attack from landward. This caught the French completely unprepared as they were arrayed for battle in the opposite fashion. Guns were manned facing out to sea but not facing in land and the British took huge advantage of this being able to fire without response for several minutes as *Goliath* followed by several ships sailed down the line pouring out broadsides as they went. By this time Nelson in the *Vanguard* had commenced the attack from the seaward side and thus the French were engaged from both sides. The French fleet was battered into submission and in the morning all but two French ships had been taken, sunk or run aground. The French flagship the one hundred and twenty gun *L'Orient* had blown up earlier in the battle with a huge explosion seen for miles and deafening those around.

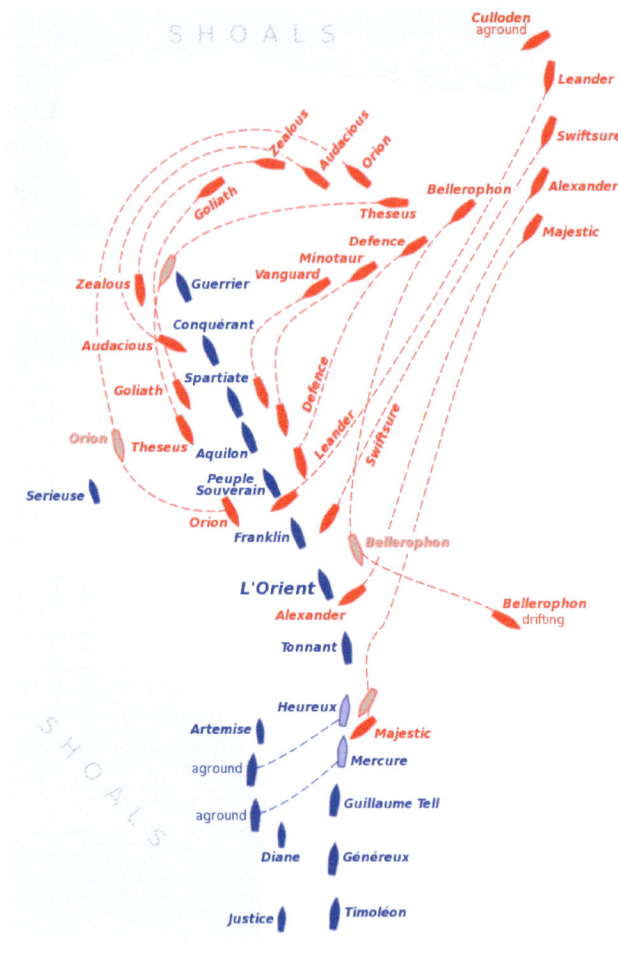

Battle of the Nile

Credit: Pinpin[5]

---

[5] Published under GNU Free Documentation License
(https://commons.wikimedia.org/wiki/Commons:GNU_Free_Documentation_License,_version_1.2) Source: https://commons.wikimedia.org/wiki/File:Trafalgar_1200hr.svg

This was a not just a victory but an annihilation, achieved not with the fighting instructions of line of battle but with independent action and initiative of Royal Navy captains. The line of battle as a tactic had now seen its day, the discipline and professionalism of the Royal Navy had reached its zenith and would go on to sweep the seas clean of the enemies of Britain. Bonaparte was now isolated and his army doomed making this a strategic victory confining the French to a land war in Europe and leaving Britain in control of the Mediterranean and able to secure further gains such as Minorca, Malta and Egypt.

Nelson's next command after recuperation in Naples and England having been wounded at the Nile was as second in command to Admiral Hyde-Parker of a fleet sent to confront a possible alliance of Russia, Sweden, Denmark and Prussia against Britain. This was a serious threat to Britain's strategic situation as a great deal of stores and timber for building warships came from the Baltic and conflict in this region against former French enemies was very much a political failure on Britain's part. The Royal Navy was blockading France and this meant stopping trade from the countries of the Baltic and Scandinavia causing much resentment. A League of Armed Neutrality was formed headed by Russia in order to enforce free trade with France and it looked as though war may well be declared by this league against Britain. In order to pre-empt any hostile action a fleet was sent to the Baltic to intimidate the members of the league and prevent aggression. The greatest fear was that when the Baltic thawed the Russian fleet could join with the Danish and Swedish fleets and present a serious threat to the Royal Navy as between them, they could muster well over one hundred sail of the line. Hyde-Parker after much pressure from Nelson decided at last to attack the Danish fleet at anchor rather than simply blockade the Baltic and dispatched Nelson to lead the attack. The Danish fleet was formidable, not many ships were fit for sea but they were arrayed in line as floating batteries and supported by batteries ashore presenting a hefty amount of firepower for any attacking fleet. In true Nelsonian fashion the British attacked on 2nd April 1801 under difficult conditions that grounded several British ships. At one stage Hyde-Parker believing the attack to be unsuccessful signalled Nelson to withdraw and discontinue the action causing Nelson to famously place his telescope to his blind eye and comment *'I see no signal'*. The action continued until the Danish having been worn down finally agreed to a cease fire and negotiations. Before these were concluded Czar Paul of Russia died and the league collapsed.

Was this a Nelson and British victory? Up until the cease fire the issue was still in doubt and could well have led to a withdrawal of the British fleet but it showed the tenacity and aggression of Nelson and the Royal Navy and alongside Czar Paul's death helped to take the momentum out of the league of Armed

Neutrality and allow Britain to continue a blockade of France and continued safe supply of goods from the Baltic.

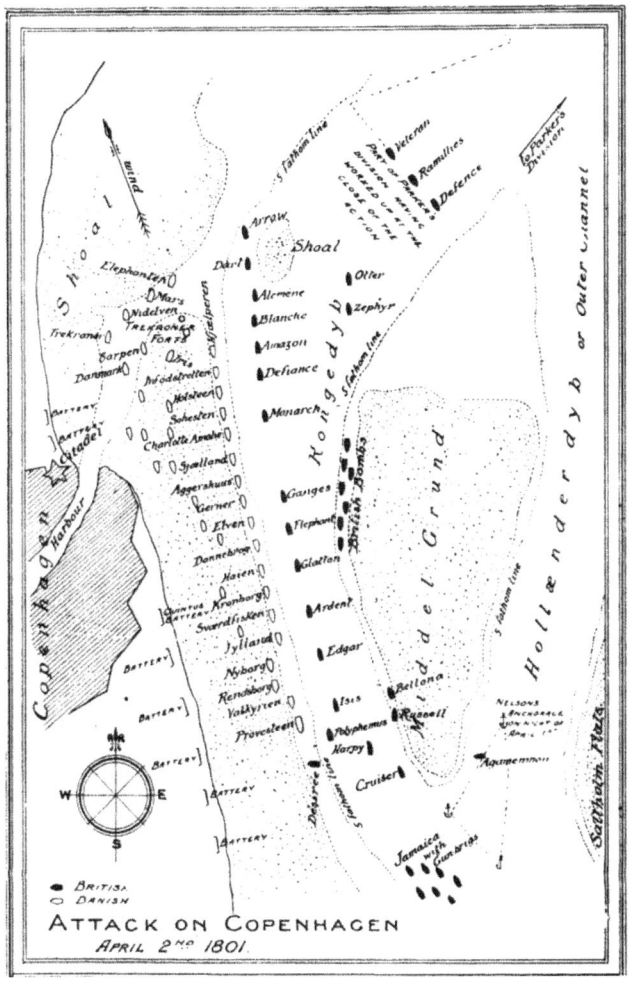

ATTACK ON COPENHAGEN
APRIL 2nd 1801.

In conjunction with the defeat of the Dutch at Camperdown and the victory at the Nile the southern and northern flanks of Europe were now secure and controlled by the Royal Navy.

With the British victorious at sea and France victorious on land a stalemate arose followed by the Peace of Amiens in 1802 which was cynically used as a breathing space certainly by Napoleon and probably by the British Government as well. The attention of the navy now turned to home waters and the new First Sea Lord Earl St Vincent decided after the mutinies of 1797 to take a good look at the corruption of the dockyards and initiate reforms to make them more efficient. Peace was very short lived however and in 1803 war broke out again between the two distrustful nations of Britain and France and blockade and convoy began again in earnest for the Royal Navy. Napoleon meanwhile was planning to do away with the old enemy of Britain once and for all and was busily constructing barges at Boulogne for an invasion of England. For two years the blockade and stalemate continued until 1805 when Napoleon considered himself ready to attempt invasion. Napoleon was not a naval man but he understood that control of the English Channel was needed for a successful invasion of England and with this in mind he gave orders that the French fleet in Toulon sail to join the Spanish at Cadiz then the fleet at Brest and enter the English Channel. This all looked perfectly simple to Napoleon but the execution was somewhat more difficult especially as the fleet at Toulon under Admiral Villeneuve was blockaded by the Mediterranean fleet under Admiral Nelson. There was a glimmer of light however for Villeneuve as Nelson's distant blockade of Toulon did give the opportunity to leave harbour and under certain conditions evade Nelson and this is exactly what Villeneuve did. Nelson learning of his departure pursued but was unsure of his destination and route finally following him all the way to the West Indies where he just missed him, they must have sailed right past each other in the Atlantic. Nelson realising that he had missed his chance sent a fast frigate back to England to report his suspicions that the fleet was headed for the Channel. This gave time for the Admiralty to assemble a scratch fleet under Admiral Calder to sail south and intercept Villeneuve off Cape Finisterre. The smaller British squadron pounded the French who lost two ships of the line but most crucially Villeneuve turned round and headed south. A disgusted Napoleon realising that invasion was now impossible and that the fleet was simply not up to what he thought the simple task of clearing the English Channel decided to move his army into central Europe and confront the Russians and Austrians instead winning a stunning victory at Austerlitz in December 1805. The threat of invasion was over for the time being but as long as the French and Spanish fleets were in being the threat remained, Nelson knew this and was determined to dispose of that threat once and for all by pursuing Villeneuve and bringing him to battle.

Villeneuve eventually led his fleet to Cadiz to join with the Spanish and combine into a formidable fleet of nearly forty sail of the line. Nelson was ordered to blockade the fleet in Cadiz and very soon after arriving he called his captains together to show them the plan of battle when the enemy came out which he was sure they would. Villeneuve did come out on the 19th October 1805 with the intention of heading back into the Mediterranean, Nelson now seized his chance and moved to intercept. As the sun rose on the 21st October Villeneuve realised that he had been spotted and attempted to run back to Cadiz, Nelson moved to attack in two columns and break the enemy line thus creating what he called a 'pell-mell battle' of individual engagements, this he hoped would lead to the capture or destruction of all the enemy ships, the annihilation he had always dreamed of.

As the fleets approached and battle became inevitable what were the thoughts of those involved? At a combined speed of about five miles an hour the crews would have had plenty of time to breakfast and lunch whilst watching the inevitable approach of battle. Fear would most certainly be prominent but also in the British sailors a sense of confidence not matched by the French and Spanish. A confidence which was shared by Nelson as his tactics suggest.

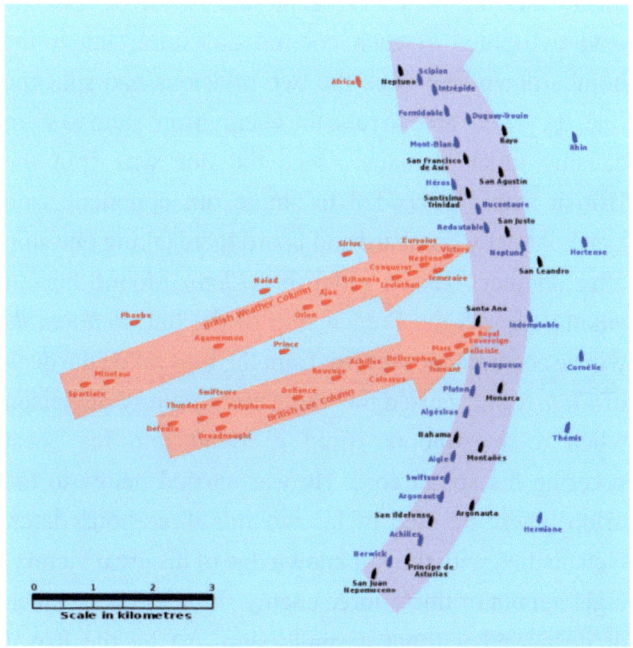

Battle of Trafalgar

Sailing in two lines right at the enemy was a risky business as it meant being a target of their broadsides for some time without being able to respond. Not as crazy as it sounds though as Nelson calculated that after months of inaction in port the French and Spanish would not be effective at sailing and fighting. No gun drill had taken place in port and as the opening broadsides came in, they were poorly timed, badly aimed and the crews very slow in reloading. On top of this the targets were the rigging, not the hulls. This meant that the men were kept safe below decks. The lead two ships of each column did suffer under the bombardment but once the two divisions had split the line, they were able to rake the enemy from stem to stern causing much damage. Once the line was split the British ships proceeded to single out opponents and systematically bombard and board them taking one ship after another. Nelson's flagship *Victory* found herself entangled with the French ship of the line *Redoutable* whose accurate musket fire from the tops raked the deck of *Victory* and caused the tragic mortal injury of Nelson when a sharpshooter fired a round into his chest severing his spinal cord. He was carried below to the orlop where he died of his wounds three hours later. Nelson died with the full knowledge of his great victory, eighteen out of thirty-three enemy ships had been taken or destroyed without a single ship lost by the Royal Navy. Nelson's last words were *'thank God I have done my duty'.*

Thus ended the threat of invasion and ultimately the eventual defeat of Napoleon on land. The supremacy of the Royal Navy had been secured and the seas would be theirs for over a hundred years. What of the death of Nelson? The death of the national hero was received with great sorrow but in terms of the navy his death had little effect unlike the death of other great commanders where we see battles and campaigns fall apart. Of course he was mourned by his men and officers but the Royal Navy had been honed to such a pitch of professionalism, discipline and aggression that the death of one man could not make a difference to its future. Trafalgar was won by the men of the Royal Navy with Nelson at its head having conceived a gallant plan of attack, but having been wounded early on Nelson was unable to influence the battle further, indeed he did not need to. Each ship and man knew his duty and what to do, in the words of Nelson *'No captain can do very wrong if he places his ship alongside that of the enemy'*. His 'band of brothers' as he called them would carry on the traditions and doctrines of Nelson and the future generations of the Royal Navy would endeavour to emulate that great fighting spirit but ultimately it was a victory for the men of the Royal Navy.

In order to complete this chapter, I do not think that a history of the Royal Navy can be complete without a brief look into its part in combating the most nefarious sea trade in history, slavery. For centuries slavers had raided the west coast of Africa to steal human cargos for work in the plantations of the West Indies and South America. The British benefitted from this in that it provided the manual labour for the growing of sugar, a cornerstone of the British economy in the 17th to 19th centuries. Indeed, those great heroes of the Elizabethan age, Drake, Hawkins and company were all slave traders and must take their place in the annals of one of our darkest periods of history.

The law in Britain at the end of the 18th century regarding slavery was ambiguous at best, however an important piece of case law called the '*Somersett Case*' was to prove a milestone in the initial moves to abolish slavery in Britain. The judgement in the case was that slavery was not supported in British common law, a major legal precedent. However, the empire was not included in this case law.

In 1793 an act against slavery was introduced in Canada and the rest of the empire was soon to follow. The main piece of legislation however was to be the Act of 1807 which outlawed the slave trade, but not slavery. However, the die was cast and Britain had put herself at the forefront of the war against this most evil of trades by establishing the West Africa Squadron whose purpose was to capture slavers plying their dreadful trade in the Atlantic.

The West Africa Squadron was formed in 1808 but due to commitments in the Napoleonic wars the squadron consisted of only two or three ships to patrol five thousand miles of coastline. In 1817 the squadron was reinforced and placed under the command of Sir Charles Collier flying his flag in the thirty-six gun frigate *HMS Creole*. Collier's orders were straight forward:

"You are to use every means in your power to prevent a continuance of the traffic in slaves".

The squadron now consisted of six ships operating out of Freetown and Ascension Island. The squadron, despite its small size, was very successful. In the fifty-two years of its operations until being absorbed into the

South Africa Command the squadron captured over sixteen hundred slave ships and freed over one hundred and fifty thousand slaves who mainly settled in Sierra Leone. One ship, *HMS Black Joke,* was responsible for taking eleven slave ships in one year, an extraordinary feat. Unfortunately, despite the squadron's efforts there were still legal obstacles to the capturing of slavers. Until 1835 only ships with slaves on board could be intercepted. This meant that any slavers clearly engaged in the slave trade yet empty could not be stopped and boarded. This also encouraged the vile act of slavers dumping their cargos overboard when a Royal Navy ship approached. In the 1840s the Royal Navy presence was greatly enhanced by the introduction of paddle steamer warships. These could not only sail against the weather but could also enter close inshore due to their shallow draft and independent power source.

The Royal Navy's efforts against the slave trade should not be underestimated. Britain stood alone in this war and showed the world how to behave. The British Empire was thus able to threaten and cajole fellow nations into changing their own laws regarding slavery. This I think is the price of being a superpower and very much a fundamental part of the *Pax Britannica* of the 19th century. One should also consider that the cost was born by Britain alone both in money and in the loss of experienced sailors. This command had a high death toll from disease and was very unpopular among the crews who faced great danger for little recognition. In modern times people have championed the idea of Britain paying reparations and apologising for her past deeds and though these arguments could hold merit the efforts of the Royal Navy and the government in fighting slavery have been forgotten. I am a huge believer in studying the past in order to learn but I hear very little if anything about the Royal Navy's and indeed Great Britain's part in the fight against slavery.

The Age of Iron and Steam — 1815 to 1914

In 1801 the first steam powered ship to be built the *Dundas* was operating on the Clyde. This was to be a major turning point in maritime affairs and one which at first the Royal Navy was reluctant to exploit. Britain still relied on her wooden walls and this was still the most economic form of warship, wind powered and able to stay at sea as long as the supplies lasted. The Admiralty did of course consider the steam engine and after the French and Napoleonic wars were over the Royal Navy began to experiment with this new technology. It was quickly realised however that coal powered ships would need constant replenishment and areas of the world would need to be turned into coaling stations which in turn had to be defended, a costly exercise, so the Admiralty came up with a compromise of paddle sloops and paddle frigates to operate close to home ports. These were not warships that were meant to take their place in the line of battle but have a far more down to earth function which was to tow the great ships of the line.

Battle of course had been foreseen for these vessels but the problem was the paddle. No matter where it was placed it was vulnerable to enemy fire and if hit could disable the ship. Just as importantly if the paddles were to the side of the ship guns could not be mounted, certainly not in any great number, reducing the firepower. Under these conditions the vast expenditure of having parts of the empire buried in coal could not be justified. One man championing one development was to change this and that was the engineer Isambard Brunel. Taking the already existing propeller from an earlier patent he created the steamer *SS Great Britain,* the first iron ship to be propelled by a screw propeller. Whilst constructing this he also composed a report on the screw propeller which was read by the Admiralty with great interest. In 1845 the Admiralty commissioned the building of a screw propeller ship the *Rattler* in order to conduct trials and see how the propeller fared against the already proven method of the paddle as propulsion. The trials showed that the propeller won hands down, even winning a tug of war with a paddle steamer as a culmination of the trials by towing it backwards. This was clearly the way forward and with paddles being replaced as a source of propulsion steam engines could be utilised in warships without any adverse effects to its fighting performance. Thus, remote parts of the empire would now became huge coal dumps to service these new engines of war.

Here begins one of the most exciting and turbulent times in the history of the Royal Navy, not in battles but in innovation where technology changed before ships were even launched and industrial practices allowed the evolution of ever larger warships to leap-frog ahead. The first ships of the line to be commissioned in this industrial age were wooden hulled ships as before but with screw propellers for use in battle or when there was no wind. Wind power was still the best form of propulsion and was still considered the main, but the writing was on the wall. In 1854 Britain went to war with Russia over the Crimea. It was during this war that the Admiralty saw the advantage that steam powered vessels had over sail in combat. During the bombardment of Russian forts in the Baltic steam powered gunboats were to prove far more manoeuvrable and able to avoid counter battery fire from shore mounted guns. This in turn led to a uniquely British form of policing the empire known as Gunboat Diplomacy.

One of the best examples of Gunboat Diplomacy that had far reaching consequences for the empire was seen during the First Opium War, a war started by Britain to reopen the previously closed trading rights with China. Not the finest hour in British history the Opium Wars were fought over tea and as the title suggests opium. For the past century or so Britain had been buying tea from China and paying for it with opium, the dreadful effects of this powerful narcotic wrought havoc in China and the trade was outlawed by the Chinese. In 1841 a naval squadron of the East India Company was sent to Canton to induce the Chinese to reopen trade with Britain. A significant member of that fleet was the ironclad paddle steamer *Nemesis*. Not a Royal Navy warship she was commissioned and built by the East India Company who were now to use her to great effect against the Chinese.

HMS Nemesis

This vessel was as yet an untried weapon of war but eyes in England were watching how she performed, one naval officer was later to write:

'The First Opium War was considered an extremely favourable opportunity for testing the advantages or otherwise of iron steam-vessels'.

And perform she did, sinking all Chinese war junks that confronted her and pursuing them up river where the shallow draft proved its worth, the Chinese coming to call *Nemesis* 'the devil ship'. Victory in the Opium War of 1841 was to provide not just a proving ground for steam powered warships but also provide Britain with one of the most lucrative and strategically important colonies in the empire, Hong Kong.

From 1855 to 1856 two hundred gunboats were built for the Royal Navy. Up to 36m long and with engines capable of delivering up to 60hp along with a full rig of sail these vessels were fast and manoeuvrable with a shallow draft perfect for inshore and river work. For armament they carried a thirty-two pounder forward and two twenty-four pounders midships, formidable armament for a ship of that size and with a crew of forty very economical on manpower. These ships proved ideal for policing the empire at far less expense and with greater speed than dispatching troops, a system that was only to change with the advent of airpower after World War I which proved even more economical. These ships could also be commanded by a lieutenant which provided an ideal command for junior officers and thus added to the experience so essential in nurturing senior naval officers, especially in a peace time navy where promotion was slow. Crews also underwent changes at this time and in 1857 we see the standardising of a uniform for lower ranks modelled on the uniform worn by sailors of the royal yacht.

Not for the first and last time the Royal Navy was confronted with challenges from contemporary navies when in 1848 the French launched the first steam powered battleship *Napoleon*. This was quickly countered by the launch in 1850 of *HMS Agamemnon*, a near copy and later by the *Duke of York* a superior vessel. Already we see the innovation we alluded to earlier begin to take shape and this in turn led to an international arms race. The next major development in naval warfare was the exploding shell which was to replace the cannonball and seal the fate of wooden warships. The French again stole a march with the introduction of the *Gloire* in 1859, the first armoured battleship. Essentially a wooden ship with armour protecting her batteries of guns firing explosive shells. *Gloire* was still wooden with all the drawbacks of a wooden warship in modern times, what was needed was a ship that could encompass all the recent technological and industrial developments and that ship was *HMS Warrior* launched in 1859. The first ironclad warship to be built with 4.5 inches of iron covering a frame of wood.

HMS Warrior

This ship which is very well known to me was the most radical action undertaken by the Royal Navy outside of war. In one stroke she rendered all other ships obsolete and became the benchmark for ship design moving forward. Able to steam at 13.5 knots she was still primarily powered by sail and her armament of twenty-eight seven inch guns and four eight inch guns (both breech loaded added in 1867 to replace muzzle loaded guns) could blow any existing ship out of the water without even coming into range of the enemy's guns. *Warrior* was the first of thirty-eight steam-powered battleships to be built in quick succession and in 1873 the first all steam powered battleship *HMS Devastation* was produced without sails and with four twelve inch guns mounted in turrets forward and midships. Albeit still muzzle loaded these turrets could individually provide a field of fire of nearly one hundred and forty degrees and set the standard for all warships moving forward. Although in its twilight years the age of sail was still not yet over and in 1870 *HMS Captain* was launched carrying both engines and sail. She was tragically to end the use of sails entirely when she capsized in a gale in the Bay of Biscay in September 1870. The reason for this maritime disaster was the simple fact that she was too low in the water having a free board of only just over six feet. She was also top heavy with sails, masts and rigging and these together with the low free board caused her to founder along with four hundred and seventy-four of her crew.

The next advance was in guns when in 1879 two battleships *Colossus* and *Edinburgh* were laid down. These would have four twelve inch guns mounted in turrets midships but unlike the earlier ships these would be breech loading guns which allowed the gun crews to be fully protected by staying within the turret.

HMS Colossus

These two superb warships were also the first to be clad in compound armour rather than wrought iron. With the introduction and improvements of armour piercing shells it became necessary to provide better armour protection and compound armour was the solution consisting of hard steel backed by tough wrought iron. This was an excellent solution to withstanding armour piercing shells. Here the pace of change slows down slightly with the launching of *HMS Collingwood* in 1880. This was to be the battleship design for the Royal Navy, with variations, for the next twenty-five years.

We now come to the question of how the men of the Royal Navy adapted to these innovations and developments and how life had changed over the past half century. In my opinion one incident can be referred to in this development and that is the tragedy of the sinking of *HMS Victoria* in June 1893. *HMS Victoria* was the flagship of Admiral Tryon, the C in C of the prestigious Mediterranean fleet. Whilst on exercise off the coast of Syria Tryon ordered the fleet to take station for the night and had its two divisions turn in on each other one coming to starboard and the other to port. A very delicate and tricky manoeuvre which needed perfect timing in its execution and plenty of sea room, at least four cables, the divisions however were only three cables apart. Here we see the dangers of manoeuvring modern fast-moving warships, as the two squadrons approached each other it was evident that the lead ship of the second column *Camperdown* containing Admiral Markham was going to ram the *Victoria*, however he continued as ordered expecting the *Victoria* and Admiral Tryon to carry out a further course change in order to avoid collision. This did not happen and *Camperdown* crashed into the starboard quarter of the *Victoria* with a sickening thud and sent her quickly to the bottom with just under four hundred of her crew who had assembled on deck awaiting instructions. The losses also included Tryon whose last words were *'it's all my fault'*. What had happened to allow such a disaster? Quite simply the Royal Navy in peace time had lost its dash and her officers had become nothing more than automatons following orders, even though as in this case they were clearly to lead to disaster. The subsequent court-martial of *Victoria's* crew split the country in two. The two sides were divided on the single issue of should Markham have followed orders (as he had done) even though they would lead to the collision or should he have disobeyed Tryon and averted the disaster. The surviving crew of *Victoria* were exonerated but Markham was not tried so no verdict was passed upon his actions. The *Victoria* verdict noted that it was difficult to condemn an officer for obeying an explicit command, but regrettable that Markham had accepted the order without query. How very different to the days of Nelson and the nurturing and encouragement of captains making decisions and feeling empowered to do so, of willingness to take risks and disobey orders for the greater good as Nelson had done at the Battle of Cape St Vincent and Thomas Foley had done at the Nile. A navy that had developed for the last half century under the heroic actions of Nelson had forgotten his one great legacy and teaching. I believe this can be put down to two things:

1. Complete mastery of the seas and no major challenges to Royal Navy power. This caused the

navy to stagnate and officers began being promoted due to length of service and seniority rather than merit. Most officers achieved very little in their careers with no war to fight and became almost administrators not having to make major decisions. War would have taken officers both good and bad of course but the throughput would be greater and more importantly promotion from the ranks would have occurred. In addition to this the service fell back into an almost aristocratic officer corps with very few seamen being promoted from the ranks and progression through merit becoming less and less likely.

2. The redundancy of sails as a means of propulsion. This in turn removed a sea captain's independence of action and thought to a certain extent but led to very well-maintained ships in order to keep sailors occupied. Cleanliness and shine became the new measure of a ship's crew and officers rather than battle training. Indeed, it has been suggested that some captains threw ammunition overboard during exercise rather than fire the guns as it would create smoke and dirt. The ship's engineers had become the most important men in the fleet yet were still considered to be interlopers in the world of a navy steeped in glory through sail. At that time an engineer officer was considered to be a non-executive officer and could not command a Royal Navy warship.

The navy would need to change and come back to its roots of an aggressive fighting force, the century was coming to a close and war was on the horizon and the Royal Navy was far from prepared for this war. Even though in the great war the navy held its own and emerged victorious the senior officer corps was woefully unprepared, however this led to the navy being in much better shape in 1939 when it was again needed in earnest.

As we have read so far in this narrative Britain was completely dependent on her trade with the empire and the Royal Navy was essential to the well-being and safety of this trade but how can they stay ahead of the other major powers and navies around the world? Strategically Britain had the advantage, she controlled key points around the globe such as Gibraltar, Hong Kong, Suez, Aden, Singapore, Ascension Island and not least of all The Falkland Islands. These key points were not just commercially far more valuable than the vast lands of the empire but they also helped the Royal Navy to control the oceans and protect trade, but only as long as it was the most powerful navy in the world and despite its size it was slowly losing ground to other nations.

The Naval Defence Act of 1889 decreed that Britain should maintain a fleet superior, or at least equal, to the next two countries in the world, at this time France and Russia. This led to an increase in shipbuilding with ten battleships and thirty eight cruisers being laid down and as the century turned the Royal Navy had forty-two battleships in commission. There was an adversary waiting in the wings however which would challenge this, not a nation but a technological invention, the torpedo. This weapon was capable of sinking a capital ship but did not need a capital ship to launch it, this meant that smaller nations could deploy fast attack craft armed with torpedoes and render a battlefleet unable to respond quickly enough to avoid them. A solution was needed and that solution became known as the torpedo boat destroyer, later simply called destroyers. Armed with guns and very fast their job was to attack torpedo boats before they got in range of launching their weapons. Soon the battlefleet would be surrounded by squadrons of these fast attack craft whose sole purpose was to protect them.

The torpedo was not to become infamous in the hands of ships but by being launched from submarines. The submarine was not a weapon that appealed to the Admiralty but they could not ignore the fact that other navies employed them and were experimenting with them and therefore in the navy estimates of 1901 provision was made for five Holland class boats. In 1902 *HM Submarine No1* was launched and was the first of this innovative weapon of war to be employed by the Royal Navy.

Holland class submarine

The submarine was here to stay and this was recognised and promoted by the new First Sea Lord Admiral Fisher. What was the submarine for though? The navy had a big gun battlefleet protected by destroyers, even if submarines accompanied a battlefleet they could not keep up with the them. Much work needed to be done but it would take a war to bring recognition for this boat as a weapon.

The Beginning of the End of Empire 1914 to 1922

Credit: historicair, Fluteflute, Bibi Saint-Pol[6]

The naval aspect of the First World War was really the clash between Britain and Germany, indeed their rivalry up to this point was very much to do with the naval arms race which played its part in the build up to war. Britain was the supreme naval power at this time, however there were contemporary navies not least of all the United States Navy who were building large warships with a view to securing trade and in America's case pushing

---

[6] Published under Creative Commons (https://creativecommons.org/licenses/by-sa/2.5/deed.en) French original: historicair, English translation: Fluteflute: Bib Saint-Pol. Source: https://commons.wikimedia.org/wiki/File:Map_Europe_alliances_1914-en.svg

potential conflict onto the oceans as opposed to fighting in the continental USA. For Britain of course the use of naval power meant an entirely different strategy. Britain's vast empire had to be defended and above all the trade routes had to be protected. For Germany the emerging dominant power of Europe a navy meant that an empire could be built. However, we go back to the fundamental problem of northern European nations throughout history in that to get to the world's oceans you must pass Britain either through the English Channel or the North Sea. As we have seen earlier in this narrative this geographical aspect was a cause of the Anglo Dutch wars and now threatened to limit Germany's empire building.

The war at sea in the great war can be divided into two main areas of activity which we will study in this chapter. The first is the clash of the surface elements of the Royal Navy and the German High Seas fleet culminating in the Battle of Jutland and the eventual starving of Germany into submission. The second is the U-boat campaigns of 1915 and 1917 to 1918, a campaign which very nearly brought Britain to its knees. When we think of the U-boat we naturally think of the Battle of the Atlantic in World War II, however in World War I the U-boat was just as big a menace and just as deadly. We will see how the Royal Navy had to adapt to an anti-submarine role as well as maintaining the traditional surface action element that had proved so decisive in the past.

Let us first look at the development of both the dreadnought and the use of blue water navies prior to World War I. In 1904 a new First Sea Lord took up his post in the Admiralty. He had served in *HMS Warrior* during the 1860s and was an expert in the use of torpedoes, thus he had a good grasp of modern technology and was to prove instrumental in the development of two classes of warship which would take their place in the annals of naval history, and contribute in their own way to the outbreak of war. His name was Sir John Arbuthnot Fisher. Jacky Fisher. Certainly, an eccentric man but most importantly a man for the time, Fisher was to shape the future and keep Britain the most powerful naval force in the world for the next fifteen years.

His first task in taking on his new role was to look at the Royal Navy dispositions throughout the empire and deploy his forces in the most efficient and strategic manor. This had to be done as a new menace was arising from across the North Sea in the shape of Germany, who under the leadership of the Kaiser and his Minister of Marine Admiral Tirpitz was threatening the Royal Navy in its own backyard. How can Britain retain the most powerful navy in the world if it cannot control home waters? This was the problem which faced Fisher, so he did three things:

1. Fisher exploited the recently concluded alliances with the Empire of Japan and France. This allowed

the bringing home of units of the fleet to be either sold off or laid up in ordinary. This meant that by 1907 the Royal Navy estimates had been reduced by several million pounds yet the fleet was more powerful and more efficient.

2. Fisher was a huge advocate of using oil in warships and pushed the government to create what we now know as BP who carried oil from the Middle East through pipelines to what was then called Palestine for use in British warships.

3. He championed and helped design two new classes of warship to beat all others. The dreadnought class and the battlecruiser.

In 1905 Japan and Russia went to war. The land campaign was fairly evenly matched but at sea Japan was in the ascendant. During the battle of The Straits of Tsushima the Japanese fleet under Admiral Togo destroyed a larger Russian battle fleet which had sailed all the way from the Baltic, thus sealing the fate of Port Arthur and ultimately winning the war. The battle was important to observers at the time as it showed how the Battleships competed and what the weapons did to armour plate. The Royal Navy consensus was that in the modern sea battle it was big guns that counted. The large ten and twelve inch guns performed very well firing with a flatter trajectory and causing serious damage after penetration. The smaller calibre guns of four, five, six and eight inches just did not count against battleships as the shells caused little damage or were of insufficient range. This vital intelligence caused Fisher to undertake the most radical designing of a warship since the *Warrior*. The result was *HMS Dreadnought* launched in 1906. She was superior in every way to any previous steam warship. She bristled with armament carrying ten, twelve inch guns in five turrets as well as many smaller calibre guns (added later to defend against destroyers) and being equipped with steam turbines giving her a top speed of over twenty knots she was almost fifty percent faster than existing battleships.

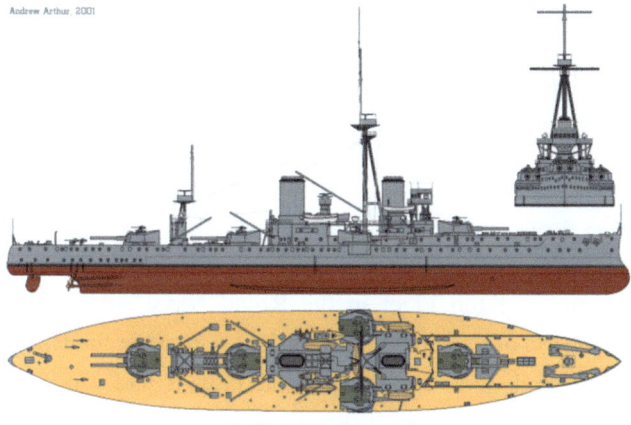

HMS Dreadnought
Credit: Emoscopes[7]

Dreadnought could both outrun and outgun any existing warship in the world. However, as a

---

[7] Published under Creative Commons (https://creativecommons.org/licenses/by-sa/3.0/deed.en) Source:
https://en.wikipedia.org/wiki/File:HMS_Dreadnought_(1911)_profile_drawing.png

consequence *Dreadnought* made almost every other battleship obsolete overnight, including those of the Royal Navy. This allowed her arch rival Germany to believe she could catch up in the naval arms race. In addition to the dreadnoughts the battle cruiser was also designed. This was not a particularly successful warship as it was never properly used for its intended purpose which was to scout ahead of the main fleet. Battle cruisers were armed with the same amount and calibre of guns as dreadnoughts, however they were considerably faster having sacrificed armour for speed. This meant that when taking their place in the line of battle they were extremely vulnerable. The concept of the battle cruiser was quite simply to scout for the fleet but have the guns to knock out opposing enemy scouts.

Kaiser Wilhelm II of the newly united Germany was obsessed with the sea. As a child he was seen and pictured many times in a sailor's uniform. He was an Admiral of the Fleet in the Royal Navy, and as the grandson of Queen Victoria he had seen what the Royal Navy had done for Britain and how it had built the empire. Germany in 1885 was a militaristic country, however this was built on an impressive and successful army. What the Kaiser understood was that if one is to build an empire, (and that was certainly his intention) one must have a navy to protect it. You cannot have one without the other. The problem was how do you convince an almost landlocked nation that its future lay in the sea?

This was a most monumental task but was achieved brilliantly by both the Kaiser and his Minister of Marine Admiral Tirpitz with a programme of education which convinced the Germans that a navy was needed and could be used. Thus, Germany began embarking on building a navy to rival its maritime neighbours, and cause questions to be raised in parliament in Britain.

The German Minister of Marine Admiral Tirpitz realised that the Imperial German Navy could never defeat the Royal Navy in an open battle, and in fairness this was never his intention. However, what the German Navy could do was apply something called risk theory, essentially this meant that all the German Navy had to do was provide a large enough threat to the Royal Navy in its own backyard. This would mean that should war occur, the British would either have to station such large numbers of ships in home waters or suffer such losses at sea in a battle (albeit at the possible destruction of the German fleet) that she could not protect her empire and its sea lanes from other enemies. Therefore, Britain would not dare fight the German Navy. Risk theory. Dangerous, but not without some merit.

Fisher's response was simple. Britain will out-build Germany. It has to be said that Fisher did his utmost to increase production of capital ships. His ultimate goal was to ensure the shipbuilding capabilities of the United Kingdom in the event of war with Germany which he prophesised would commence in October 1914 after the completion of the Kiel Canal. As it happens, he was not far wrong except that the Kiel Canal was finished several months earlier than expected. The canal had but one purpose, to allow the passage of shipping including warships from the Baltic to the North Sea without having to go around Denmark and into the guns of the waiting Grand Fleet. This was considered a provocative action by Fisher and many in Britain and would help fuel the fires of potential conflict. At this time the Liberal government was very committed to the beginnings of a welfare state with the provision of pensions and unemployment benefits. Fisher played on the nation's fears and this was picked up by the popular press who demanded more dreadnoughts. Press headlines ran 'We want eight and we won't wait'. These were controversial times and with dreadnought expenditure topping the nation's defence budget the government had to juggle defence expenditure and popular feeling which is never easy, as Churchill at the time quipped *'The Admiralty wanted six, the economists wanted four so we settled on eight.'* Eight was something that Germany just could not compete with. At the outbreak of war Britain had twenty dreadnoughts with a further twelve under construction, Germany had fifteen and six under construction. However, it should be noted here that there were two dreadnoughts under construction for the Turkish Navy in British dockyards in 1914 and on the outbreak of war the Admiralty seized these for the Royal Navy. An act which would cause resentment in Turkey and help drive the Turks into the arms of the Central Powers, especially after Germany gave Turkey a battlecruiser and a light cruiser on the outbreak of war.

What Tirpitz and the Kaiser did not count on with risk theory were three things. Firstly, the recall of ships from the Far East, increasing Royal Navy strength in home waters. Secondly, the simple fact that Britain could out-build Germany in dreadnoughts and thirdly the British reaction to the out brake of war and the strategy employed which was quite simply to stand off and blockade Germany. Tirpitz and the Kaiser were expecting an immediate attack on its North Sea bases through heavily mined and submarine patrolled waters, a Copenhagen type manoeuvre was expected as in Nelson's battle of 1801. It didn't happen. The Germans now had a choice. If they come out, they will be annihilated, if they stay in port Germany would starve. The Germans didn't know what to do.

Attention now shifts to the oceans of the world rather than British home waters with the only substantial clash of British and German warships outside of the North Sea in what history has called the battles of Coronel and the Falklands. On the outbreak of WWI, the German Asiatic Squadron under the command of Admiral Graf Von Spee found itself in Tsingtao cut off from German home waters. The spectre of conflict with Japan also raised its head so Von Spee did the only thing he could do and set sail for home across the Pacific. The squadron was quite formidable in terms of light forces with two armoured cruisers *Scharnhorst* and *Gneisenau* and three light cruisers *Dresden, Leipzig* and *Nurnberg*. No dreadnoughts but a sizeable squadron with the potential to disrupt Britain's trade routes. This worried the Admiralty whom assumed that this was precisely what Von Spee would do so a scratch squadron under Admiral Craddoc was assembled to intercept and destroy Von Spee.

Battle was joined 1st November off the Chilean coast near Coronel. The Royal Navy squadron was completely outclassed and outgunned and was destroyed. The only survivor was the light cruiser, *Glasgow*, which sailed to join the pre dreadnought battleship, *Canopus*, at the Falklands Islands and at least provide some protection for this vital outpost. This defeat created a dangerous situation for Britain as it left the entire South American and South African trade routes open to attack by Von Spee who could well have exploited the situation. However, he failed to do so, commerce raiding was not at the forefront of German maritime thinking at this stage of the war but it was most certainly a missed opportunity as events twenty-five years later in another war would prove. Instead, Von Spee after resting his crews and carrying out minor repairs off the South American coast decided to carry out a raid on the Falkland Islands and destroy the wireless station and coal supplies.

The British response to this outrage of a defeat of a Royal Navy squadron, the first in over one hundred years, was to seek revenge, the initiative in the naval war must be taken back and above all the Falklands protected. To this end a squadron under Admiral Doveton Sturdee was dispatched to the Falklands comprising two battlecruisers and for light cruisers crucially reaching the islands before Von Spee who had a nasty shock when he approached the Falklands on the 8th December. Whilst concentrating his fire on the *Canopus* Von Spee did not see until the last minute the two battlecruisers steaming out of East Falkland from behind the hills which hid them from the German Squadron and all too late he realised he had sailed into a deathly trap. Von Spee realising he could not outrun the battlecruisers ordered his two armoured cruisers to engage whilst the light cruisers scattered and made their way independently to the nearest neutral port. Both armoured cruisers were sunk and two of the light cruisers were engaged and sunk by the British Light Cruisers. *Dresden* survived but was caught three months later and sunk. This engagement though small compared to Jutland was equally significant. It protected the sea lanes for Britain and confined Germany to home waters for the remainder of the war.

The main conflict was always going to be in Europe where the two huge fleets glared at each other over the brooding waters of the North Sea. The Royal Navy stood off and blockaded the German coast from afar but did venture out to attack German ships and to raid when appropriate. The first such clash took place on the 28th

August when a light squadron of two cruisers and two destroyer flotillas backed by the battlecruiser fleet caught light German forces off the Dogger Bank sinking three light cruisers and sinking and damaging several Destroyers, precursor to the main events of 1915 and 1916.

The Battle of Jutland was a fascinating battle in many respects. But two aspects stand out for me. Firstly, it represented the last major confrontation of surface fleets without the aid of aircraft carriers, secondly it was an important battle in that for the first time, heavy dreadnought class battleships had faced each other. Looking back to the days of sail one could safely predict that British seamanship, gunnery and aggressive boarding would win the day against enemy ships. However, in the dreadnought age the chances of carrying an action by boarding would not be an option. As we shall discover gunnery was more than ever of importance but rather than rate of fire it was the way in which guns were managed. In the age of sail where the British Navy fired three broadsides to every one of the enemy at close range, the effect was devastating. However, in the age of dreadnoughts the rate of fire was not only less important as opposed to accuracy, but was to prove fatal to British warships.

Thus was the position in 1914 after war had broken out. The Royal Navy was based in Scapa Flow carrying out a standoff blockade of Germany whilst protecting its own sea lanes. The Germans now had to decide what to do. A vast amount of money had been spent on the navy and the people expected some return. In addition to this the army was becoming resentful of the fact that they were fighting and dying on two fronts and the navy did not appear to be doing anything. The German fleet also wanted action however the Kaiser was loathed to risk his beloved ships in a major confrontation with the Royal Navy. And so, the German Navy was to embark on the policy of hit and run. The purpose of this strategy was for the Battlecruiser Squadron (with the High Seas Fleet in support) to carry out raids on the seaside towns of England and draw out part of the Grand Fleet, probably the Battlecruiser Fleet which had become more autonomous under Beatty and lead it into the guns of the main fleet and destroy it. Thus, inflicting disproportionate attrition to wear down the Grand Fleet. The initial attempts at this strategy were only partly successful in that seaside towns such as Scarborough were shelled but the Germans withdrew too quickly for the Royal Navy to catch them.

What the Germans were not aware of however was that the code breaking section known as Room 40 (based at the Admiralty in London) had cracked German codes and were aware of some of the movements. The Germans knew that there was a security problem somewhere, however they assumed incorrectly that intelligence was being gathered by the British fishing fleets off the Dogger Bank so in January 1915 the 1st Scouting Group of Battlecruisers under Admiral Hipper swept into the Dogger Bank with a view to destroying the fishing vessels. The Royal Navy of course was tipped to this by Room 40 and the inconclusive Battle of Dogger Bank was fought with the result that the Germans were chased back to home waters having lost an armoured cruiser the *Blucher*.

The battle was not terribly important as far as losses and tactical advantage was concerned, however it did highlight the difficulties of trying to control large numbers of warships in a battle. Flag signalling was still in use by the Royal Navy (little different from Nelson's time) only with the additional problems that a modern fleet gives, such as visual problems with thick acrid smoke in the air from guns and engines, higher speeds and of course greater distances. The German battlecruisers escaped because the British, not seeing the signals properly or misinterpreting them, concentrated their fire on one ship, the *Blucher*. This situation was also not helped by the Fleet Commander Admiral Beatty having to leave his flagship *HMS Lion* after she was hit. In the intervening time it took to move his command to a cruiser the battle had moved on and the battlecruisers rather than picking individual targets had instead concentrated their fire on the *Blucher*. The *Blucher* herself was not an important target, she was an armoured cruiser (pre-dreadnought) placed with the 1st Scouting Fleet simply because there was nowhere else to put her.

On the 30th May 1916 Room 40 intercepted intelligence which it understood to mean that the High Seas Fleet (or at least part of it, most likely the 1st Scouting Fleet) was preparing to leave harbour for a sortie into the North Sea. Jellicoe ordered the Grand Fleet and the Battlecruiser Fleet (with the 5th Battle Squadron of the new fast *Queen Elizabeth* class battleships attached) to leave port with a view to joining up near Jutland and conducting a sweep. However, by midday on the 31st it was not clear which German units had left port. This was because the Admiralty had intercepted radio signals from Scheer's flagship which put her still in port. However, this code prefix was later identified as the code for the Admiral when at sea, not in port, so the appearance later of the High Seas Fleet would be as big a surprise to Jellicoe as the appearance of the Grand Fleet was to Scheer.

At 14:40 on the 31st May, the advance screen of Royal Navy cruisers spotted smoke to the east and after investigating further *HMS Galatea* signalled to Beatty 'enemy in sight', it was Hipper's 1st Scouting Fleet. Beatty ordered a turn to the South South East in order to cut off Hipper and the opposing fleets began to converge. Here we see one of the poor command decisions of Beatty in that he opened fire at around the same time as Hipper when the bigger guns of his battlecruisers could in fact have opened fire earlier. At around 16:10 disaster struck for the first but not last time that day when the *Indefatigable* suddenly received hits from a salvo (probably fired by the *Von Der Tann*) and promptly blew up. Only two seamen of the nine hundred crew survived. Disaster struck again at 16:26 when the combined fire of *Seydlitz* and *Derflinger* caused the *Queen Mary* to also explode killing all but twenty of her twelve hundred crew. This caused Beatty to make his famous remark to Ernle Chatfield *'there seems to be something wrong with our bloody ships today!'* There was. Not in the ships but in the handling of them in action. As noted earlier the Royal Navy was all about gunnery and rate of fire. This policy caused numerous mistakes to be made in the fire control of British warships, most notably: Flash doors were left open to make the passage of shells and cordite faster and charges were left piled on deck ready for use. With all this together a hit on a turret (any turret) and the flame would pass right through to the magazine causing a massive explosion.

By this time the 5th Battle Squadron had now begun firing on the German battlecruisers when Admiral Goodenough in the light cruiser *Southampton* spotted the High Seas Fleet coming up from the south east. Beatty promptly turned north west in order to lead them onto the approaching Grand Fleet.

The battle now moved to the hopefully decisive phase of the two main battle fleets engaging. Jellicoe's first decision was to release Admiral Hood's 3rd Battlecruiser Squadron to assist Beatty. Whilst this was underway Beatty withdrew from Hipper whose attention was turned to the 5th Battle Squadron. This squadron was still steaming south under Beatty's orders, no doubt surprised to pass his fleet moving the opposite way! Beatty had failed to relay his instructions to the squadron.

At 17.35 Beatty once more turned into the 1st Scouting Fleet in order to drive them off course away from the Grand Fleet, thus depriving Scheer of his eyes. At this time the 1st Scouting Fleet was also engaged by Hood's 3rd Battlecruiser Squadron which had run into them by mistake. The resultant fighting ended in the loss of the German light cruiser, *Wiesbaden*.

At 18.15 Jellicoe deployed his fleet from heading south east to heading east. This was probably the most important naval decision ever made in the Great War. Jellicoe was still uncertain as to the whereabouts of the High Seas Fleet. Beatty had still not given any indication of the course and speed of Scheer, most likely being too engrossed in his own battle and forgetting his primary purpose which was as a scouting group for the main fleet. Thus, Jellicoe had to make the most important decision of his career based on the last reports of Beatty's position and the sound of gunfire. It was the correct decision and allowed the Grand Fleet to cross the enemy's 'T'.

At 18.22 Scheer steamed right into any German admiral's worst nightmare, a one on one with the Grand Fleet with his 'T' crossed. Meanwhile Hipper sheared off pursued by Beatty and Hood. It was at this time that the third heavy loss of the day befell the Royal Navy when *Invincible* blew up in the same fashion as the previous two battlecruisers.

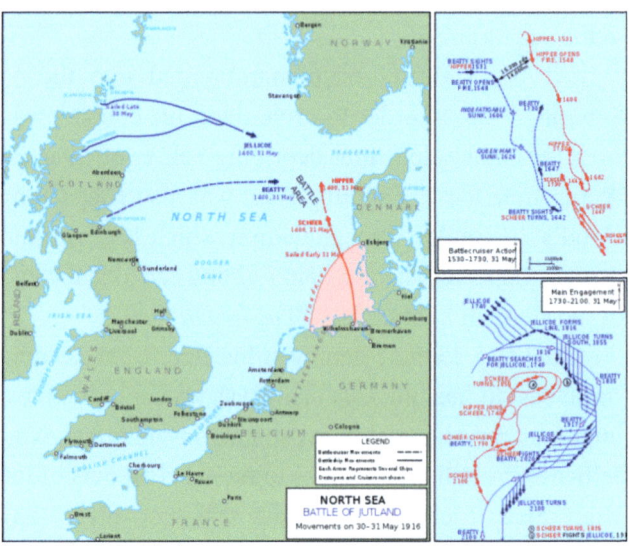

Credit: Grandiose, rowanwindwhistler[8]

For fifteen minutes the Grand Fleet pounded the leading battleships of the High Seas Fleet causing severe damage, yet not sinking a single battleship. This is a tribute to the design and construction of the German ships. Scheer then ordered a brilliant manoeuvre and all ships turned one hundred and eighty degrees and

---

[8] Published under Creative Commons (https://creativecommons.org/licenses/by-sa/4.0/deed.en) Source:
https://commons.wikimedia.org/wiki/File:Map_of_the_Battle_of_Jutland,_1916-es.svg

reversed course disappearing into the haze. However, twenty minutes later Scheer ordered an about turn and headed back into the Grand Fleet. This order has caused much historical argument as it was an almost suicidal manoeuvre. The best guess is that Scheer was either hoping to cross the Grand Fleet's rear and cross its 'T' or most likely he was hoping to bypass the Grand fleet entirely and sail around them back to Germany whilst Jellicoe looked to the westward. In any event the only way out this time after another severe pounding was for Scheer to launch a mass torpedo attack from his destroyers whilst he turned the battle fleet away once again. This is where the historical debate really begins. Jellicoe's standing orders were quite clear in the event of a torpedo attack, the fleet will turn away. This is what he ordered thus allowing the Germans to escape.

This was the end of the major fleet action. That night there was sporadic fighting as the fleets intermingled in the darkness and this action resulted in the loss of numerous destroyers and cruisers on either side as well as the elderly German pre-dreadnought, *Pommern*. Again, communication was not forthcoming from the forces engaged and another opportunity to engage was missed.

The losses in the battle were heavy, certainly in lives lost. The British lost three battlecruisers, three armoured cruisers and nine destroyers along with around 8,000 men. German losses were one battlecruiser, one pre-dreadnought battleship, four cruisers and five destroyers with around two thousand five hundred men. Certainly, tactically the Germans had won the day by dint of killing more men and sinking more ships. However, battles (and certainly naval battles) are not judged on losses. They are judged on who commands the sea afterwards. In this respect the Royal Navy was victorious as it commanded the sea and continued its blockade of Germany. The Grand Fleet was ready for sea again twenty-four hours after returning to port, whereas the High Seas Fleet would not be able to put to sea again for some months due to the extreme damage inflicted on them in the encounter. Indeed, some ships would never put to sea again. It should also be noted that the Germans barely escaped and did so only due to British standard procedures in the face of torpedo attack followed by later communication failures. When Tirpitz reported to the Kaiser he said we must never do this again or we will be destroyed.

Historians and leading figures after the battle have all attempted to dissect the engagement and apportion blame for the failure of the Royal Navy to make a better showing of itself. Some (including Beatty) have sought to change history and make Jellicoe the scapegoat for what they considered a rather mediocre performance by the Grand Fleet. Others have sought to lionise Jellicoe for his masterly handling of what was a very difficult set piece battle. I am of the latter school of thought and I will give my reasons why.

1. The job of the battlecruiser as envisaged was not to take position in the line of battle, it was to act as the eyes of the main fleet and report enemy course and speed. However, from the early days of WWI the Battlecruiser fleet under Beatty had come to act more autonomously and separate from the North Sea Fleet. Of course Beatty engaged Hipper in the best traditions of the Royal Navy, however having become engrossed in his own battle he became lax in reporting the movements of the High Seas Fleet to Jellicoe, thus leaving him to make an educated guess as to its course and speed. Beatty also failed to include the 5th Battle Squadron (which was attached to his command) in his orders and movements. This not only deprived him of five of the most powerful and advanced battleships in the world, it also caused them to run into enemy forces at a disadvantage. In the years after the battle Beatty was instrumental in having Jellicoe removed as the C in C of the Grand Fleet and he clearly re-wrote history to cover himself and lay blame at Jellicoe's door for the perceived poor performance.

2. Jellicoe's decision to deploy during the battle was perhaps the most important and bravest order ever given in a sea battle. Without the intelligence of Beatty he judged through experience and knowledge of the sea when and where to deploy.

Had he been wrong the Germans would have crossed his 'T' to his rear causing huge damage. One must put oneself in Jellicoe's shoes and realise that he was the only man who could lose the war in an afternoon. The most controversial order of the day was for the fleet to turn away from the torpedo attack. Again, the right decision. This was criticised by Beatty after the battle. However, it should be remembered that Beatty did exactly the same thing at the Dogger Bank a year earlier. Torpedoes had proved to be devastating weapons and could well have severely damaged or sunk a dozen battleships. The object of the battle was not just to destroy the enemy but to keep the seas and force the Germans back to port whilst keeping the Grand Fleet in being.

The Battle of Jutland was not of course the only naval battle of WWI, but alongside the vital defence of the trade routes over the North Atlantic it was the most important. Whereas the victory over the German submarine arm was essential to Britain's survival, equally the holding at bay and neutralising of the German surface fleet was vital to Germany's defeat.

Historians now, in light of the centenary celebrations especially, are looking at this battle in more detail and especially its part in the winning of the war. Modern technology has allowed historians and archaeologists to investigate the ships sunk and the damage done adding more evidence to the already known effects of poor handling of munitions and the rapid-fire doctrine of the Royal Navy at that time. For my part to reiterate my earlier thoughts I would go so far as to say that this battle was instrumental in the defeat of Germany. Of course the final offensives of 1918 on the western front broke the back of the German Army but it was a German Army that was starving and what little food Germany had was taken from the civilian population in Germany, this in itself caused low morale in the army as soldiers worried about their families back home.

The battle of Jutland could well have cost Britain the war had she not retained possession of the seas. Equally it caused the defeat of Germany through old fashioned blockade which in the 20th century proved just as potent a weapon as it had ever been.

At the beginning of the war both Britain and Germany had submarines. For Britain they were very much an experimental class of warship designed more to help understand the threat rather than as an offensive weapon. In Germany the *Unterseaboot* or U-boat was seen as a possible leveller in the war against the Royal Navy. As discussed in the previous chapter it was hoped that the Grand Fleet would venture into German waters where U-boats and mines would hopefully take their toll. Indeed, within weeks of war being declared we see early German U-boat victories.

On 22nd September 1914, three elderly Royal Navy armoured cruisers of the 3rd Cruiser Flotilla were patrolling off the Dogger Bank when they were all sunk one after the other in quick succession by U9. A particularly sad happening as only a day before the First Lord of the Admiralty Winston Churchill had ordered that the squadron be withdrawn as it was in unnecessary danger and not contributing to the blockade. This attack was followed later in the year by the torpedoing of the cruiser, *HMS Hawke*, the seaplane carrier, *HMS Hermes*, and an elderly pre-dreadnought battleship. The submarine was making its mark but not without loss. U11 was sunk by a mine, U15 rammed by the cruiser, *Birmingham* and U18 sunk trying to enter the Grand Fleet anchorage of Scapa Flow, (an operation emulated in 1939 with far greater success). At the end of the year, one could consider the results even. British ships had been sunk, mainly elderly but three U-boats were also sunk. Germany started the war with only thirty-five such craft and had suffered nearly ten percent losses already for no major gain.

In April 1915 U-boats were sent to the Mediterranean to help the Turks in the ill-fated Dardanelles campaign where they sunk two pre-dreadnoughts *HMS Triumph* and *Majestic* however for all these sinkings of British warships the U-boat arm was not diminishing the Grand Fleet and its ability to fight and out-gun the German High Seas Fleet. The High Seas Fleet could still not come out and challenge the Royal Navy for control of the seas and commerce was continuing as goods made their uninterrupted way into British ports. Could the U-boats be used to combat this trade?

International maritime law at this time was very clear on the engaging of merchant shipping in time of war. Basically, if a ship was suspected of carrying military contraband it could be stopped, boarded then allowed to be sunk after the crew was safely put into lifeboats. Not a job for a submarine so Germany decided to consider unrestricted U-boat warfare. This plan had its champions and detractors, the navy of course were all for it as they could see that severing Britain's lifelines was essential to victory on land, no different to its own blockade by the Royal Navy. However, the politicians were far more concerned over the repercussions of such actions on world opinion. The German Chancellor Bethmann-Hollweg was violently against this new direction the war may take fearing the United States could be brought into the war against Germany. Feelings in the United States were already turning against Germany after reports emerged of German atrocities in occupied Belgium early in the war and this worried the Chancellor greatly. The final decision would of course come from the Kaiser who overruled his Chancellor and on 16th February 1915, a zone around the UK was proclaimed by the German Government and any ship in that zone was liable to attack by the German Navy.

There were mixed results from this initial U-boat campaign. In the six-month period that the unrestricted campaign lasted nine hundred thousand tons of merchant shipping were sunk, however this figure was more than balanced out by the British dockyards producing over two million tons of merchant shipping. This initial campaign also saw several key developments in both anti-submarine warfare and, as we shall discover, world opinion. The sinking of merchant ships caused the Royal Navy to adapt to a new type of warfare where the enemy was virtually unseen and undetectable, how does one fight this? Patrol and hunting groups were set up in the sea around the UK consisting of elderly destroyers, armed trawlers and Royal Naval Air Service (RNAS) Dirigibles. Hydrophones were also invented, these could detect the noise of a propeller over some distance and depth charges used to attack U-boats under the surface, the first depth charge kill being recorded in July 1916. In addition to these measures the Dover barrage consisting of mines and later a steel net was created to close off the English Channel to U-boats in 1915 between Dover and Calais.

Despite being under sea craft, in the early years of war U-boats carried out their attacks on the surface using either the deck gun or torpedoes. It was far easier to attack on the surface as when dived the speed diminished and if the gun was used it conserved torpedoes. This strategy gave the Royal Navy for a limited period of time a unique deterrent against surface attack, what were called 'mystery ships', more commonly known as Q-ships. These were merchant ships packed with guns which were hidden both within the structure of the merchant ship and on deck, the idea being when a U-boat surfaced to carry out its attack it would meet with a hail of fire. This system was augmented by the installation of guns on merchant ships but by mid-1916, U-boats had become wise to the dangers of surfaced attack and carried out their war under the ocean.

As we have seen this unrestricted campaign did not achieve great results and thanks to the sinkings of the *SS Falaba* and the *Lusitania* in Spring 1915 US public opinion swiftly turned against Germany and this barbaric form of warfare. It was certainly true that Britain was blockading Germany at the same time and this also caused unrest in the US but it should be remembered that Britain did not attack merchant shipping. It boarded ships and took any appropriate cargo after paying for it, a huge difference. This first unrestricted campaign had however shown that the submarine could be a potent weapon in the war against trade. Had the numbers of U-boats which were later seen in 1917 been available the tonnage sunk would have been far greater and potentially led to the defeat of Britain, one of history's great 'what ifs'. In any event the unrestricted warfare was called off after six months.

By the end of 1916 it was clear that Germany was on the road to defeat in the great war. On the western front German divisions were outnumbered by the allies having only one hundred and fifty divisions to the Allies one hundred and ninety, they were still fighting on two fronts and the British blockade was beginning to tell with the first cases of malnutrition being recorded in Germany. In December 1916 the German Navy again raised the tactic of unrestricted U-boat warfare and presented a report to the Kaiser claiming that if six hundred thousand tons of allied shipping was sunk a month Britain would starve. To counter the threat of US intervention the report went on to say that Britain could be starved in six months, long before the US could react decisively with military intervention and should the US continue to involve herself militarily the navy could stop any troops landing on the continent of Europe. There was equally huge disquiet in Germany, especially from the army, in the perception that the navy for all its vast expenditure pre-war was not doing anything significant to aid the war effort. Unrestricted warfare was very much an all or nothing policy but it gave the German Navy an opportunity to reassert itself. At a high command meeting in January 1917 Hindenburg declared *'The war must be brought to an end by whatever means as soon as possible'*. Unrestricted submarine warfare was reinstated on 1st February 1917.

The first months of the campaign brought startling success and seemed to justify the faith of the German military and the Kaiser. By the end of June 1917 well over three million tons of merchant shipping had been sunk with only nine U-boats lost and at one stage Britain was down to only six weeks' worth of grain. The allied convoy system was now coming into its own however and losses dwindled for the rest of the year never exceeding five hundred thousand tons a month and mostly hovering around three hundred thousand tones, well within sustainable levels. The Allies also set up the Allied Maritime Transport Council which worked to ensure that all available shipping was used to carry the correct commodities and products to Britain which made sure that the convoys delivered the most essential products in the most economic fashion. The true victor in this battle however was the convoy system. Convoys were not popular at first and the Admiralty was not keen to use them as they created problems of control whilst at sea especially at night. They foresaw a lack of cooperation from merchant ship captains and difficulties in coordination. Convoys were also reduced to the speed of the slowest ship present which often meant a crawling pace. Not insignificantly the convoy system also went against the grain of the Royal Navy in that it was considered to be too defensive minded, a far cry from the aggressive nature the navy had fostered over the centuries. Royal Navy captains wanted to attack enemy ships, not plod along on the fringes of convoys seeing little if any action. But for all these drawbacks a convoy had two distinct advantages.

Firstly, it was hard to spot a convoy at sea, just as hard as a single ship, especially from the very low profile of a submarine either surfaced or submerged. The Atlantic is a big ocean with huge tossing waves most of the time, very easy to hide. Secondly, you can protect a convoy with escorts and these escorts proved decisive in finally beating the U-boats. At the end of 1917 over one hundred U-boats had been lost and German production simply could not keep up with this loss rate. Most importantly of all the United States entered the war against Germany in April 1917 bringing within a year a vast army that was to prove decisive.

When war finally ended in November 1918 the German High Sea Fleet was brought into Scapa Flow and interned whilst peace negotiations were carried out in Paris. The German fleet would no doubt be part of any final agreement and was likely to be dismantled as it had been deemed to be a major contributor to the outbreak of war. Thus, as history records it was scuttled by its crews. What of the Royal Navy? It had conducted itself with its usual professionalism, courage and ingenuity to see Britain through what had been its darkest hour in over one hundred years but it was not the victory that had been expected of it. Only one major fleet action had been fought which was a tactical defeat, albeit a strategic victory, but this did not sit well with the public. Indeed, the king also expressed dismay over the failure of the fleet to destroy the enemy. Even Jacky Fisher who had retired from the navy by the time of

Jutland expressed his dismay at the failure of the Grand Fleet to destroy the German High Seas Fleet at Jutland. To my mind a greater victory was won by the Royal Navy than any fleet action. It had blockaded Germany and starved her into submission. It had allowed the safe transportation of troops from the empire to fight in France, ultimately allowing for the free passage of the United States Army to France, all of which helped defeat Germany on land. The Royal Navy had adapted to a new dangerous form of warfare with the threat from under the sea and had both kept Britain from starving and allowed supply of important war materials. With the advent of the U-boat campaigns the Royal Navy had been forced to adopt an entirely new form of warfare for which it was neither designed, prepared or equipped yet unlike its cousins on land it pragmatically won that battle. This complete change of tact through need was not to be seen again until the Falklands War of 1982 when conversely an anti-submarine navy was forced to fight a conventional war and land an army.

With the ending of the Great War the Royal Navy had to face its sternest test yet by learning the lessons of that war and coming to terms with the fact that in that war the navy was pushed into second place by the army as the key arbiter of victory, certainly in the eyes of the British public. Despite the appalling casualties on the western front and the complete lack of direction from the senior generals the victors such as Haig were seen as heroes whereas the navy having been unable to carry out a Trafalgar like victory at sea were seen as having failed in their duty. Of course this is not the case as the earlier narrative shows, the navy played its part in the defeat of Germany but without the elan and dash of the previous centuries. Where were the Nelsons, Drakes and Rodneys? Jellicoe had proved to be a competent commander but lacking in imagination. Beatty, perhaps the closest to the Nelsonian spirit had shown gusto but his ability was questionable. What the nation had failed to grasp and what I have tried to put across in this book is that winning battles is just a part of the role of the Royal Navy through history. Granted an important part but only one of the building blocks of empire. It was the navy's presence throughout history as a constant that allowed the empire to function and grow and throughout World War I this is exactly what the navy had done.

How do we now come to the end of our story by suggesting that the end of the war was the start of the decline of empire? Quite simply three reasons, one is the near bankruptcy of Britain after the war and the inability to retain a navy of the size previous to the conflict. Second is the rise of the US Navy and the supplanting of Britain by this new industrial and financial powerhouse and thirdly the political changes in Britain and her colonies after the war. Let us look at these in more detail.

After the war both Britain and the United States embarked on large ship building programs both planning new large super dreadnoughts and accompanying battlecruisers. The United States was of the firm belief that trade causes wars and with that in mind it now began to look upon Britain as the next enemy in the next war, Britain in turn considered the United States to be a potential enemy. Luckily this joint expansion did not continue as lessons were finally learned from the arms races of the past, especially before the Great War. Both sides decided to look at alternatives which was a huge relief to Britain who simply could not afford to keep up. The Washington Treaty of 1922 was the solution to the growing naval arms race around the world and it was agreed by all signatory nations that Britain and America would have parity in numbers of capital warships. This was offset to some extent by other nations such as Japan and Italy being limited to the number of warships they could have and we see the magic 5:5:3 formula in capital ships being agreed. Put simply for every five capital ships owned by Britain and the United States, Japan, Italy and France could have three. This still allowed for a supremacy, enough to protect the empire, but the days of huge battlefleets were over. In addition to these restrictions ship classes were limited to tonnage, for example thirty-five thousand tons for a battleship, ten thousand tons for a cruiser. War still came of course in 1939 after the political failures of the Treaty of Versailles and the Washington Treaty did not prevent World War II. This is absolutely true of course and might even have accelerated war by creating resentment among certain nations but we can I think thank the treaty for perhaps preventing a great Anglo-American war in the 1920s. Despite all this however after over two centuries of naval supremacy with the sweep of a pen Britain gave up her prominence of being the number one naval power in the world to the nation that had supplanted her as the primary industrial and commercial nation in the world, the USA, a changing of the guard not just in a naval sense but industrially and above all financially as we see after the war the main financial centre of the world moving from London to New York.

After the war British politics changed with a view that the fleet had not achieved a great deal in the war and therefore was it needed in such strength? Britain, who had always protected the empire, really could not afford to do so any more and we see in the 1920s and 30s the rise of commonwealth navies such as the Royal Australian Navy, Royal New Zealand Navy, Royal Canadian Navy and the Imperial Indian Navy. The role of the Royal Navy was to change in that she retained the battlefleet and all the responsibilities that came with that, but the smaller colonial navies would become more prominent in their part of the world. British naval commitment overseas reduced, rather in the same way as Fisher had done at the turn of the century but on a much larger scale. By the mid-1920s the Royal Navy had gone from forty-five battleships to just twenty and would start the next war in 1939 with only fifteen battleships and battlecruisers.

The British Empire, like most other empires in history, did not die in a violent cataclysm of war and conquest, but merely ceased to exist of its own volition over a period of the next fifty years or so. The previously subject peoples and countries no longer really needed the empire and had, through the violent bloodletting of the Great War, earned the right to autonomy or independence. Britain, for her part, was in no condition to resist the steady break-up of the empire, but she did retain a Commonwealth of countries, some sharing the head of state of the British royal family. This was perhaps the best outcome for all concerned; the world was changing and the Great War was a landmark occurrence which led directly to the end of the old empires and the rise of the new empires of the USA and the Soviet Union. Not perhaps empires in the old sense of conquest and between Britain and her former colonies, but more in ideology and influence. The Commonwealth did, however, allow close ties between Britain and her former colonies, ties which are still strong today. I always liken this in basic form to a toasted cheese sandwich. One bites into it and pulls away a great chunk of mass but no matter how hard one bites, the strands are still there connecting the main bodies. This is perhaps the greatest epitaph of any empire.

Epilogue

In the 21st century the Royal Navy is still a presence in the world. After the Falklands War of 1982 there was no more mention of the navy being just an anti-submarine force in the North Atlantic, she would continue to be a power for good in the world and her reach and scope is now as deadly as it was at any time in history. In this brief narrative we have seen the Royal Navy fight extraordinary battles but there has also been much innovation and development which all navies and civilian ships have profited from.

This narrative was concerned only with the years up to the beginning of the end of empire for Great Britain but the navy still lives on with all its traditions and history. As I write this there are two huge carriers which have recently been commissioned that equal in size the US Navy carriers giving the Royal Navy a reach far in excess of our own waters.

HMS Daring and HMS Dauntless
Type 45 Destroyers
Credit: LA(Phot) Ian Simpson

These carriers will be protected by Type 45 destroyers and Type 26 and Type 31 frigates, the most technologically advanced warships in the world. The Royal Navy is also the custodian of Britain's submarine launched nuclear deterrent Trident, which will be updated over the next fifteen years, continuing the threat of assured second strike capability and one trusts giving the ever-growing number of countries who now possess nuclear arms a pause for thought. We must also consider the humanitarian work of the Royal Navy. Whenever a disaster occurs in the world a Royal Navy ship is often the first on scene helping to organize local resources to get things back on track. Royal Navy warships patrol the drug trafficking lanes of the Caribbean and have had much success in stopping contraband. They patrol the sea lanes around East Africa and help the international effort to combat modern day piracy.

HMS Queen Elizabeth, credit: Martin Wraight

However, as I write this my mind cannot help but think that the real difference made by the Royal Navy today is that she is an expression of our political will. One looks at the recent controversial wars around the Middle East and we see a huge US presence in firepower and hardware. Alongside it is a Royal Navy complement. This shows the extent to which this country is ever the loyal lieutenant of the United States and will doubtless continue to be so for good or ill. Our presence alongside her gives her moral and diplomatic strength which has a major effect on what the United States does around the world, which perhaps poses the question if we did not have the special relationship would the US be so active on the world stage?

Whilst writing this book I have learned a great deal. My knowledge of certain periods was already in being and helpful but my further research has given me a great insight into how important the Royal Navy was and continues to be to the world, not just the nation.

Glossary

Aircraft carrier – *Warship designed to hold, launch and recover warplanes from a specially designed deck*

Armored Cruiser – *See Cruiser. Has a band of armor along the sides as well as armored decking*

Battle Cruiser – *See Cruiser. Designed with Battleship caliber guns but with cruiser armor. It's task was to behave as a conventional cruiser but be able to blast enemy cruisers and scouts out of the water to deprive the enemy of their 'eyes' at sea.*

Battleship – *A term used to denote a large warship with many and/or large calibers of guns. In the age of sail it would be called a ship of the line*

Brigade – Army formation of usually three to five battalions or regiments.

Bloody Code – 18th and 19th century laws which carried an instant death penalty if transgressed.

Cable – Measurement of length used at sea., about 185 meters.

Carrier – *See Aircraft carrier*

Catapult – *Steam powered accessory on a carrier to*

propel a warplane off the deck. Designed by the Royal Navy

Chaff – *Defense aid for countering homing missiles aimed at ships or aircraft*

Chasers – Cannon located in the bow and stern of a sailing ship

Commando – *From the Boer term meaning fast land striking force, in this book describers Royal marine Commandos.*

Crossing the T – *Term used to describe the preferred maneuver when warships cross a line of enemy warships at a 90-degree angle bringing all guns to bare on the enemy ships.*

Cruiser – *Postindustrial fast warship of moderate gun caliber used for escort, scouting and convoy protection.*

Destroyer – *Postindustrial warship originally designed to combat Torpedo bots. In modern warfare an escort vessel for anti-submarine and air defense purposes.*

Dreadnought – *Named after HMS Dreadnought launched in 1906. This term describes all post Dreadnought battleship designs.*

Dry dock – *where a ship can be built or maintained whilst out of the water*

Exocet – *French built anti shipping missile both air and sea launched.*

First rate – *Category of battleships used by the Royal Navy in the age of sail denoting a battleship with three decks and over 100 cannons of various caliber.*

Flagship – *Ship containing Admiral or Commodore of a fleet, squadron or flotilla*

Fleet – *A large collection of ships. In military terms the equivalent of an army*

Fleet Air Arm – *Air component of the Royal Navy*

Flotilla – *Group of small sized warships*

Frigate – *In preindustrial times a fast warship of up to 36 guns used for patrolling, commerce raiding and escort duties. In modern warfare generally an anti-submarine and air defense warship*

Galleass – *hybrid of a galley and a galleon with heavy cannon in the bow mostly employed in the Mediterranean*

Galleon – *mainly commercial ocean-going ships with*

cannon for protection, often double up as warships until the mid-17th century

Landing ship – *Purpose built craft for facilitating landing of troops on a shore. It would be the mother ship of smaller craft used to carry the troops ashore whilst providing command and control facilities.*

Line astern – *Formation used for both battle and movement of large numbers of warships*

Line of Battle – *Traditional formation of battleships from mid-17th century*

Marines – *troops fighting on board ships and attached to the navy*

MI6 – *Military Intelligence Department 6, Britain's Secret Intelligence Service.*

Mine – *High explosive charge that sits under on the surface of a sea or waterway detonating when a ship passes over it of comes into contact with it.*

Minesweeper – *Warship used to detect and remove mines*

NATO – *North Atlantic Treaty Organization formed in 1949 for defense of the west against Soviet aggression.*

Pieces of eight – A Spanish silver dollar to the value of eight reales

Pre-Dreadnought – *See Dreadnought. Describes battleships built before launch of HMS Dreadnought in 1906.*

Privateer – *Pirate ship with a letter of marque from a sovereign or nation to prey upon enemies or potential enemies*

Race built galleon – *smaller than a galleon, heavily armed with raised fore and aft decks*

RFA – *Royal Fleet Auxiliary, provides maritime support for the Royal Navy*

Sail/Ship of the line – *Commonly used to describe battleships that take their place in the line of battle*

Scurvy – A disease arising through lack of vitamin C. Common in the age of sale due to the lack of fresh fruit and vegetables aboard ships. The Royal Navy countered this with the use of citrus fruits, this in turn led to British seamen being called 'limies' by Americans especially.

Sea Dart – *Long to Medium range radar guided homing anti-aircraft missile fitted to Royal Navy Type 42 Destroyers during Falklands conflict.*

Sea Wolf – *Short range anti-aircraft missile fitted to Royal Navy Type 22 Frigates during Falklands conflict.*

Second Rate – *See First Rate, Second rate battleship comprised two decks with up to 98 guns. A British invention not entirely successful as they proved poor sailors being very ungainly.*

Ship Money – A tax traditionally levied on coastal towns but under Charles I collected inland and without the permission of Parliament. One of the factors that led to Civil War.

Squadron – *A collection of ships too small to be called a fleet*

SSK – *Submarine Submersible Killer, modern nuclear hunter killer submarine*

Submarine – *Pre-Nuclear age a ship able to remain underwater for limited periods. Able to attack with torpedoes enemy ships whilst submerged.*

Third Rate – *See First rate, Third rate ships carried 64 - 74 cannons on two decks. Main ships of most navies in the age of sail*

Torpedo – *Long, cylindrical, propelled, underwater missile with an explosive charge attached.*

Torpedo boats – *Fast moving attack craft armed with torpedoes*

Total Exclusion Zone or TEZ – *Military confinement zone placed around the Falklands by the Royal Navy inhibiting all naval and air movement in and out of the islands*

U-boat – *See Submarine. German Submarines, Unterseeboot*

VSTOL – *Vertical Straight Take off and Landing, applied to the Hawker Harrier*

Weather Gauge – From the age of sail. Being up-wind of an enemy vessel giving initiative over the enemy vessel in terms of speed and positioning.

INDEX

Aboukir Bay, 96
Admiralty, 41, 64, 66, 73, 81, 89, 90, 93, 95, 103, 111, 112, 113, 123, 127, 132, 134, 137, 139, 153
American Revolutionary War, 70
Anglo-Dutch Wars, 33
Asiento, 48
Austerlitz, 103
Baltic, 99, 101, 113, 128, 132
Batavian Republic, 93
Beachy Head, 42, 43, 44
Black Prince, 17
Bombay, 38
Bonaparte, 96, 99
Boulogne, 102
Cadiz, 22, 31, 52, 85, 87, 102, 104
Calais, 19, 26, 150
Camperdown, 81, 94, 95, 102, 119
Cape Horn, 58, 60
Caribbean, 48, 49, 50, 58, 162
Charles I, 30, 31, 36, 38, 40, 42, 46, 169
Charles II, 36, 38, 40, 42, 46
Chatham, 37, 44
Chesapeake Bay, 71, 75
Copenhagen, 82, 133

Coronel, 133, 134
Crimea, 113
Deptford, 25
Dreadnought, 129, 165, 168
Duke of York, 35, 36, 38, 42, 116
Dundas, 111
Dungeness, 34
East India Company, 28, 36, 38, 113
Egypt, 96, 99
Elizabeth I, 19
Falkland, 122, 134, 135
First Lord of the Admiralty, 62, 72, 148
First Opium War, 113, 114
Frigate, 90, 166
George III, 71, 73
Gibraltar, 46, 47, 51, 85, 122
Gloire, 116
Glorious Revolution, 42
Gunboat, 113
Harwich, 34
Henry VIII, 17, 23, 44
Jamaica, 75, 77
Jutland, 126, 135, 136, 139, 142, 146, 147, 155
Kentish Knock, 33
Kiel, 131
Latitude, 63

League of Armed Neutrality, 99
Longitude, 65
Lord Admiral, 16, 51, 124
Lowestoft, 36, 37
Marines, 35, 45, 46, 167
Mary Rose, 18, 19
Medina Sidonia, 23, 27
Medway, 25, 37, 77
Mutiny, 64
Napoleon, 80, 102, 106, 115
Naval Defence Act, 122
Navigation Acts, 33, 38
Navy Board, 18, 25, 37, 40
Nemesis, 114
New France, 50, 56
North Devon, 17
Pax Britannica, 81, 109
Plymouth, 17, 25
Portobello, 49, 50
Portsmouth, 35, 45, 73, 89
Quiberon Bay, 51, 53, 54, 56
Rattler, 112
Royal Charles, 37
Scurvy, 60, 168
Seven Years War, 50, 54, 56, 69, 70, 84
Somersett Case, 108
South Sea Company, 48
Sovereign of the Sea, 30, 31, 32
Spithead, 81, 89, 90, 93
SS Great Britain, 112
Submarine, 123, 169, 170
Torbay, 42, 53
Toulon, 51, 52, 96, 102
Ushant, 25, 51, 53, 82
Washington Treaty, 157
West Indies, 38, 69, 71, 72, 75, 77, 90, 103, 107
William of Orange, 42
Wrecks Act, 65